William Forsyth

The Slavonic Provinces South of the Danube

A Sketch of their History and Present State in Relation to the Ottoman Porte

William Forsyth

The Slavonic Provinces South of the Danube
A Sketch of their History and Present State in Relation to the Ottoman Porte

ISBN/EAN: 9783337412166

Printed in Europe, USA, Canada, Australia, Japan

Cover: Foto ©ninafisch / pixelio.de

More available books at **www.hansebooks.com**

THE

SLAVONIC PROVINCES

SOUTH OF THE DANUBE.

A SKETCH OF THEIR HISTORY AND PRESENT STATE
IN RELATION TO

THE OTTOMAN PORTE.

BY

WILLIAM FORSYTH, Q.C., LL.D., M.P.,

Author of "The Life of Cicero;"
"Cases and Opinions on Constitutional Law,"
&c., &c.
LATE FELLOW OF TRINITY COLLEGE, CAMBRIDGE.

WITH A MAP.

LONDON:
JOHN MURRAY, ALBEMARLE ST.
1876.

BY SAME AUTHOR.

HORTENSIUS; an Historical Essay on the Office and Duties of an Advocate. Second Edition, with Illustrations, 8vo. 12s.

LIFE AND TIMES OF CICERO; His Character as a Statesman, Orator, and Friend. With a Selection from his Correspondence and Orations. 3rd Edition. With Illustrations, 8vo. 10s. 6d.

THE NOVELS AND NOVELISTS OF THE 18th CENTURY; in Illustration of the Manners and Morals of the Age. Post 8vo, 10s. 6d.

HISTORY OF ANCIENT MANUSCRIPTS. Post 8vo, 2s. 6d.

PREFACE.

So little is really known in this country of the past history and present state of the Slavonic Provinces of Turkey, and the information to be got is scattered in so many volumes—most of them in foreign languages—that I thought it might be useful to bring the salient points within the compass of a short notice, and thus assist in forming a correct judgment upon a question, which is, by the irresistible logic of facts, forcing itself upon public attention, and which I believe is destined, if not now effectually dealt with, to be a source of ever-recurring trouble to the peace of Europe.

CONTENTS.

I.

THE SLAVS.

I.

THE SLAVS.

By the Slavonic Provinces fouth of the Danube I mean Servia, Bofnia with the Herzegovina and Turkifh Croatia, Montenegro, and Bulgaria.

There are other Slavonic provinces to which the fame geographical definition applies, fuch as Croatia proper, Slavonia between the Save and the Drave, and Dalmatia; but thefe do not come within the fcope of the prefent notice, for they belong exclufively to Auftria, and the Ottoman Porte makes no pretenfions to dominion over them.

The Danubian Provinces of the Roman Empire in the fecond century of the Chriftian era

were known under the general names of Dacia
on the north of the Danube, and Mœsia, Pannonia, and Dalmatia, on the fouth. But the
whole of this fouthern region was generally called
Illyricum. Dacia comprifed the modern provinces of Moldavia and Wallachia, now known
as Roumania, north of which were the vaft
deferts of Sarmatia or Scythia.* Mœfia, which
was divided into Superior and Inferior, contained
part of Bofnia, and the whole of Servia and Bulgaria. The reft of Bofnia was in Pannonia, and
Montenegro is part of the ancient Illyricum or
Dalmatia, the name given to the ftrip of coaft
on the eaftern fea-board of the Adriatic. The
whole of thefe provinces were known as the
Illyrian frontier of the Roman dominion, and
were efteemed, as Gibbon fays, the moft warlike
of the Empire. The Dacians he calls the moft

---

* *Sauromatas gentes Scytharum Græci vocant, quos Sarmatas
Romani*, Plin. Hift. Nat. lib. 4, c. 11. Florus fays of the inhabitants, *Tanta barbaries est ut pacem non intelligant*, lib. 4, c. 12.

warlike of men. Dacia was conquered by Trajan after a memorable ftruggle of five years. It had been invaded previoufly by Domitian, and although he did not really fubdue it, he gratified his vanity by a triumph.

The traveller, who like myfelf in 1869 defcends the Danube, will, on entering the magnificent fcenery of the Carpathian gorge, obferve on the right bank of the river, about ten feet above the furface of the water, a long feries of fquare holes in the lofty rocks of Servia, extending for nearly fifty miles, as far as the Iron Gates. For ages the origin of thefe holes remained a myftery, and puzzled antiquaries, many fanciful theories being fuggefted to account for them. But they are now afcertained beyond a doubt to be the fockets in which were inferted the wooden crofs-beams upon which were laid planks to form the great military road called the *Via Trajana*, along which the Roman legions marched. It muft have been a work of immenfe

5

labour, and is one of the many proofs of the indomitable energy and engineering ſkill of the conquerors of the world.

Gibbon, who publiſhed the firſt volume of his Hiſtory in 1776, ſays,* " The inland parts (of " Illyricum) have aſſumed the Slavonian names " of Croatia and Boſnia ; the former obeys an " Auſtrian Governor, the latter a Turkiſh " Pacha ; but the whole country is ſtill infeſted " by tribes of barbarians, whoſe ſavage indepen- " dence irregularly marks the doubtful limit of " the Chriſtian and Mahometan power." This deſcription is not applicable at the preſent day. The inhabitants are certainly not barbarians, and neither Croatia nor Boſnia is independent—the one belonging to Auſtria and the other to Turkey.

The real origin of the Slavs is loſt in the darkneſs of antiquity. Guided, however, by philology, which is the only ſure key that un-

* Decline and Fall, chap. 1.,

6

locks the myſtery of the primeval relationſhip of different nations, we know that they were a great offſhoot of the Aryan family of man; *
and hiſtory tells us that when they appeared in Europe they dwelt or roamed in the boundleſs ſteppes of Scythia and Sarmatia before they ſpread weſtward, croſſed the Danube, and over-ran the provinces of the Roman Empire. The name is ſaid to be derived from *Slava,* which in the Slavonic language ſignifies Glory ; but the people muſt have had a diſtinctive name, before by their warlike deeds they could arrogate to themſelves the title of Glorious, and therefore we cannot conſider it as their *original* appellation.†

* A reference to Bopp's Comparative Grammar (*Vergleichende Grammatik*) will ſhow how intimately the Slavonic language is connected with Sanſcrit, or rather is derived from it.

† Another derivation is from *Slovo,* word or ſpeech, to diſtinguiſh the nation from the races whoſe language it did not underſtand. So the Greeks called foreign nations Βάρβαροι, "Barbarians," which had special reference to language. Βαρβάρους, ἀντὶ τοῦ ἀφώνους.—Suidas.

ἐγὼ γαρ αὐτοὺς, βαρβάρους ὄντας προτοῦ,
ἐδίδαξα τὴν φωνὴν —Ariſtoph. Aves.

Procopius (de Bello Gothico, iii. 14), who wrote in the fixth century, fays that the Slavs were anciently called Spori, becaufe they occupied land with tents fcattered far apart. This, however, is clearly a falfe etymology, for Sporadic, which means "fcattered," is derived from a Greek word, a language of which the Slavs then knew nothing.* He generally mentions them in connection with the Antes, a tribe whofe conqueft by Juftinian induced the Roman emperor to add Anticus to his other titles. And Jornandes, Bifhop of Ravenna, who was a contemporary of Procopius, fpeaks of the Slavs (Sclavini) and the Antes as the principal nations of Scythia, and as dwelling in marfhes and forefts inftead of towns.† According to Herder,‡ they were firft met with on the Don, then

---

* A not improbable derivation of Spori is from *S'bor*, pronounced *Sabor*, the Slavonic word for council or affembly.

† *Hi paludes fylvafque pro civitatibus habent.*—Jornandes, De Rebus Geticis, cap. 5.

‡ Ideen zur Philofophie der Gefchichte der Menfchheit, Vierter Theil, p. 31.

8

amongſt the Goths, and afterwards on the
Danube, amidſt the Huns and Bulgarians—
preferring to obtain quiet poſſeſſion of lands
evacuated by the Teutonic tribes, rather than
gain them by force of arms.

Slavonic writers, ſuch as Schafarik, are fond of
repreſenting their countrymen in the olden time
as a quiet inoffenſive people, only too happy to
be at peace with their neighbours. But there
really ſeems to be no authority for this, and it is
much like the dream of a former Golden Age—
for certainly, when the Slavs firſt appear on the
ſtage of Hiſtory, we find them a reſtleſs, warlike,
and aggreſſive nation.

With regard to their origin, the truth ſeems
to be that the Slavs were an agglomeration of
various tribes united by the tie of a common
dialeƈt, of which Sanſcrit is the oldeſt known
form. Their Indian or Aryan deſcent is ſhown
not only by their language, but alſo by one or
two curious cuſtoms which prevailed amongſt

9

them, and which no doubt they inherited from their Afiatic progenitors. One of thefe was the practice of *Suttee*, for their widows ufed to burn themfelves on the funeral piles of their deceafed hufbands. Now, although it is true that futtee is not mentioned in the Vedas,* nor in their ancient commentator Menu, and hence fome have inferred that widow-burning is a later innovation, it is recognized in the epic poetry of the Hindus, and was common amongft feveral of the Aryan nations. Another cuftom was the principle of undivided family, which exifts in full force amongft the Hindus at the prefent day. " Equal divifion fprings from the moft " ancient conftitutional principle of the Slavs— " that of joint and undivided family poffeffion, " and periodical fharing of the produce ; this " probably exifted among all the Slavonian races,

* " The burning of widows was not enjoined in the Vedas, " and hence, in order to gain a fanction of it, a paffage in the " Veda was falfified."—Max Müller, Chips from a German Workfhop, vol. iv. p. 318.

" and is ftill to be found in Servia, Croatia, &c.,
" where it is the practice in fome parts not even
" to divide the land every year, but to cultivate
" it jointly under the direction of the ' elders,'
" and only to fhare the harvefts equally among
" the elders of the commune."* In Servia, at
the prefent day, there is an inftitution called
Zadrouga, which is defined in the Servian code
to be " a community of living and property
" founded on relationfhip." The oldeft living
anceftor is called *Stareschina*, and all who are
defcended from him work for a common purfe
under his direction and management. But the
affociation is voluntary, and any member is at
liberty to withdraw from it, juft as in India
" feparation " frequently takes place, and the
undivided family becomes divided.†

---

* Haxthaufen's Ruffian Empire, vol. i. p. 120.

† " In Servia, in Croatia, and the Auftrian Slavonia, the
" villages are alfo brotherhoods of perfons who are at once
" co-owners and kinfmen."—Ancient Law, by Sir Henry
Maine, p. 267.

Procopius tells us that the form of government amongſt the Slavonians was a democracy, and they deliberated in a public aſſembly.* But we are not to ſuppoſe from this that there was one aſſembly for the whole nation, for there were numerous ſubdiviſions, each of which ſeems to have been independent of the other, and the old name for the petty chiefs was *Zupan*, the original meaning of which is "ſunny land." They were as cruel as they were brave, and we learn from ancient writers with what ingenious barbarity they tortured their captives taken in war. Gibbon, in his uſual ſtyle of heſitating and qualified aſſertion, ſays that the cruelties of the Slavonians are "related or magnified" by Procopius, but there ſeems no reaſon to doubt that what he tells us of them is true. A good deſcription of their phyſical appearance is given by Count Kraſinſki, and is, in fact, an epitome of

* οὐκ ἄρχονται πρὸς ἀνδρὸς ἑνὸς, *i.e.* they had no ſingle ruler.—Procop. de Bell. Goth. iii. 14.

the accounts we find in the old Greek and Latin
authors.

" The ancient Slavonians are defcribed as tall
" and of very ftrong make ; their complexion
" was not very white, and their hair was of a
" reddifh colour. They could eafily fupport
" hunger, thirft, heat, cold and want of covering,
" and were dirty in their habits. They lived in
" miferable huts, and they often changed their
" place of abode. They went into battle without
" fhirt or cloak, and their only covering was a
" pair of fhort troufers." *

In the great Slavonic overflow that rufhed
like a torrent over part of Europe, fome portions
of the race fpread themfelves through the paffes
of the Carpathian Mountians to the weft and
north as far as Poland and Pomerania, and the
Czechs of Bohemia are part of the fame nation

* Quoted by Sir G. Wilkinfon in his " Dalmatia and Montenegro," vol. i. p. 34. Except as regards the troufers the defcription might apply to the Highlanders of former days.

that fettled in the countries on the fouth of the
Danube. The total amount of the Slavonic
population in Europe now, is eftimated at not
lefs than eighty millions.* This is a fact with
which Europe will one day have to reckon.
They are fcattered over the continent, and in
fome parts fo intermixed with other races that it
is difficult to diftinguifh them. The only geographical divifion which has obtained or kept the
original name of the nation is Slavonia, the
country between the Save and the Drave, both
affluents of the Danube, and which belongs to
Auftria.

It is to the fouthern immigration of the race
that I fhall confine myfelf in the following
notice.

* Deutfches Staats Worterbuch.   Die Slaven, Band ix.

II.

SERVIA.

II.

SERVIA.

SERVIA ought to be pronounced Serbia. The softening of the *b* into *v* is suggestive of a wrong etymology, as if it had some connection with the Latin word *Servus*.* But inveterate habit has taught us to speak of Servia, and so it is written in all the Consular Reports received at the

---

* And yet the word " slave " is supposed to be derived from the Slavs, and to have originated in the eighth century in the eastern part of France, where the princes and bishops had many Slavonian captives. " From the Euxine to the Adriatic, in the " state of captives or subjects, or allies or enemies, of the Greek " Empire, they (the Slavonians) overspread the land; and the " national appellation of the *Slaves* has been degraded by chance " or malice from the signification of glory (*flava*, laus, gloria) " to that of servitude."—Gibbon, Decline and Fall, chap. 55. The old Slavonic word for *flave* is *rab*.

Foreign Office.* I fhall therefore ufe the word Servia, although under proteft.

The moft powerful Slavonic tribe that croffed the Danube and fettled itfelf on the fouth of that river was the S'rbi or Serbi, fometimes written S'rbli. Their name feems to have been applied in old times very generally to the whole Slavonic people. This immigration was in the feventh century. At that time the favage hordes of the Tartar Avars had devaftated the northern provinces of the Greek Empire, and fettled themfelves in Macedonia. The Serbs were invited by the Emperor Heraclius to come and expel thefe intruders, and when they had done this, they foon afterwards marched northwards and fpread themfelves over the country now known as Bulgaria, Servia, and Bofnia, great part of which had previoufly been occupied by

---

* The proper name of Servia is S'rbia, and the Servians are in Slavonic S'rbs ; but the neceffity of pronunciation compels us to infert the *e*, juft as we are obliged to turn the Slavonic word *S'bor*, council or affembly, into *Sabor*.

the Getæ and Triballi. Gradually they extended their poffeffions both weft and fouth, and the Servian hiftorian, Davidovitch, enumerates thirteen territories now known under diftinct names which were once under the dominion of his countrymen.* According to Conftantine Porphyrogenitus the Servian people embraced Chriftianity in the reign of the Emperor Heraclius, but it is believed that their converfion took place at a later epoch. We know that the Scriptures were tranflated into the Slavonic tongue by St. Cyril and Methodius fome time in the ninth century, and this is ftill the facred language of the Slavonic nations which are members of the Greek Church. The Serbs were governed by chiefs called Zupans, and it was not for fome time that thefe fubmitted to the authority of a fingle ruler called Veliki or Grand Zupan. Indeed it is not clear that at firft the Grand Zupan was more than *primus inter pares*,

* Les Serbes en Turquie, par Ubicini, pp. 24, 25.

and in the old Slavonic language he was called *Starjefina* or Senior, and had his refidence at Deftinika on the Drina, which feparates Servia from Bofnia. In the tenth century the Zupan of Dioclea raifed himfelf to the chief power. In the meantime the Servians acknowledged the fupremacy of the Greek Empire, but made it a condition that they fhould remain under the rule of their own Zupans, who were elected by the free choice of the people. They were long engaged in bloody ftruggles with their neighbours, and in the year 924 the Bulgarians who occupied the territory to the eaft, and of whom I fhall fpeak more particularly hereafter, invaded Servia and completely conquered it. Many of the Servian nobles were fent as hoftages into Bulgaria, and a great part of the population was tranfplanted there, while the land was ravaged and laid wafte by the Bulgarian hordes.* This was while Symeon was ruler of Bulgaria, but

* Schafarik, *Slavifche Alterthümer*, ii. 31.

after his death the Servians, with the help of the Greek Emperor, recovered the territory they had loft, and their Grand Zupan Tcheflav renewed his homage to the Greek Court. This feudal relationfhip became complete dependence after the overthrow of the Bulgarian kingdom by the Emperor Bafil II. in 1018, and Servia was treated as a province of the Greek Empire. But in 1040-43 Stephan Bogiflaw, who had been imprifoned at Conftantinople, effected his efcape, and returning to his native country expelled the Greek governor and reftored Servia to a ftate of independence. And when in 1043 the Greek Emperor Conftantine Monomachus fent a powerful army to attempt the conqueft of Servia, it was met by the Servians in the mountains, and annihilated in their impaffable defiles. Bogiflaw's fon and fucceffor Michael took the title of king or *kral* of the Servians, and as fuch was acknowledged by Pope Gregory VII. (1073-78).

We need not follow in detail the obfcure

history of the Servians and their struggles with the Greek Empire, but come at once to Stephan Nemandia, Zupan of Rafcia, who was raifed to the throne in 1165, and became the founder of a powerful dynafty, the feat of whofe government was at Rafcia, now Novi Bazar. He was of the family of the Zupans of Dioclea, and ruled for thirty-fix years with vigour and fuccefs, confiderably enlarging the extent of his dominions. At laft he abdicated the throne and became a monk, dying in a monaftery of Mount Athos, in the year 1200.

He was fucceeded by his fon Stephan, who was furnamed Pervovenfhani, " firft-crowned king," although, as we have feen, the kingly title had been affumed by earlier rulers; and the crown was worn by fucceffive members of the Nemandia family until it came to Stephan Dūfhan (1336–1358), under whom the Servian Principality or kingdom rofe to its greateft height of power, and embraced the largeft extent of terri-

tory—including not only Servia proper, but
Macedonia, Theſſaly, and Albania, and alſo
Bulgaria.* With him, ſays Schafarik, the certain hiſtory of Servia begins.† With the aſſent
of the *Sabor*—an aſſembly of the principal chiefs,
which, on ſpecial occaſions, formed the Parliament of old Servia, he aſſumed the title of
Czar.

In his reign (1349) a code of laws was
enacted in an aſſembly at which were preſent
" the Patriarch, the Metropolitans and the
" Biſhops, the Czar, the *Kniezes* or *Knees*, and
" the greater and leſſer governors of the
" empire." Theſe laws conſiſted of 105 articles,
and it may be intereſting to cite a few of
them.

They provided for the maintenance of Chriſtian

---

* Schafarik, *Slaviſche Alterthümer*, ii. 32.

† Ranke (Hiſtory of Servia) ſays, " A complete and authentic
" Hiſtory of Servia cannot be expected until writings, ſuch as
" Domitian's Life of St. Simeon and St. Sava, and the Rodoſlow
" of the Archbiſhop Danien and his ſucceſſors, are publiſhed, and
" with a correct text."

worſhip and the extirpation of hereſy. Converts to the Latin Church, on refuſal to return to the orthodox faith, were to be puniſhed with death. No layman was to act as a judge in eccleſiaſtical affairs. The Church alone was to decide in Church matters. Church property was not to be alienated. The Churches were not to be ſubordinate to the Great Church (of Conſtantinople). A nobleman who affronted the honour of another nobleman was to pay a fine. But a mere gentleman who did ſo was in addition to be flogged. A nobleman who violated a married woman was to have his hands and noſe cut off. The adultery of a married woman was puniſhed by the loſs of her ears and noſe. A nobleman not invited to a repaſt was not to intrude himſelf by force ; but if invited he was to be punctual, or he was guilty of an offence. All meetings of peaſants were forbidden under the penalty of mutilation of ears and branding. Diſputes between different villages were to be

settled by an appeal to the Czar. The burning
of corpses was forbidden. Wilful murder was
punished with loss of hands, but if the murdered
man was one of the clergy, with death. Parri-
cides and infanticides were to be burnt. Whole
neighbourhoods were made responsible for theft.
Brigands and robbers were to be hanged. Ad-
vocates in courts of justice were not to calum-
niate their opponents. Judges were to deliver
written judgments, and give copies to the
parties. Drunkenness was severely punished:
drunkards who made a riot or committed an
assault were to have their eyes torn out and one
of their hands cut off. A widow was not to
marry again until a decent period of mourning
for her former husband had elapsed. The wife
of a soldier engaged in war was to wait ten
years, unless she had written news of his death,
before she could contract another marriage.

Stephan Dūshan assumed the proud title of
Czar of the Serbs and Greeks, and even aspired

to the throne of Conftantinople itfelf. In the conteft for the imperial purple between John Palæologus and John Cantacuzene, the latter had invoked and obtained the aid of Stephan. The Servian ruler was at this time a powerful monarch, and he made it a condition of his alliance that whatever towns were taken fhould have the liberty of choofing either himfelf or Cantacuzene as their fovereign. Gibbon does not mention this ftipulation, but he defcribes the attitude of the two monarchs. " The *Cral* or " defpot of the Servians received him (Cantacu- " zene) with generous hofpitality ; but the ally " was infenfibly degraded to a fuppliant, a hoftage, " a captive ; and in this miferable dependence " he waited at the door of the barbarian, who " could difpofe of the life and liberty of a Roman " Emperor."* The ill-afforted alliance, how- ever, did not laft long. Jealoufies broke out, and Cantacuzene miftrufting Stephan fought for

* Decline and Fall, chap. 63.

other fupport. He called to his aid the Ofmanli Turks, who had invaded Afia Minor, but had not yet croffed the Bofphorus. Thus came about "the paffage of the Ottomans into Europe " —the laft and fatal ftroke in the fall of the " Roman Empire." *

Stephan Dūfhan feems to have been a true "Αναξ ἀνδρων, leader of men, tall of ftature, and of commanding prefence. Gibbon is quite wrong in calling him a barbarian. He overran nearly the whole of what is now called Turkey in Europe, and befieged the Emperor Andronicus in Theffalonica, compelling him to cede Macedonia. Afterwards he turned his arms northwards, and defeated Louis, King of Hungary, in feveral battles. Having quarrelled with Cantacuzene, as I have already mentioned, he marched upon Conftantinople at the head of a large army, but was feized with fever at Devoli and died there in 1358.

* Decline and Fall, chap. 63.

He was fucceeded by his fon Urofch, who was murdered by one of the Servian chiefs, and he was the laft of the Nemandia dynafty in the direct line. On his death in 1357, the people chofe, or the crown devolved upon, Lazar, who was related to the Nemandia family, and he became king or *Cral* of Servia. The memory of none of their rulers lingers more fondly in the hearts and fongs of the people than that of this unfortunate prince. He was brave and juft and generous, but fortune hardly ever fmiled upon his arms. In a conteft with the Hungarians he was defeated and deprived of the royal title, and was obliged to content himfelf with the inferior dignity of *Knes*. And when, in 1389, the Sultan Amurath I. invaded Servia, he had to fight a laft defperate battle for the independence of his country.

Alarmed at the rapid approach of the Turks, Lazar looked round for help, and appealed to the rulers of Bofnia, Hungary, and even

Poland to aid him in the ftruggle. But no effective affiftance came, and he had to bear the brunt of the ftorm almoft alone. The two armies met in the Plain of Kóffovo, and the Servians were utterly defeated. Lazar fell in the battle, but at the fame moment, or indeed juft before, the Sultan Amurath perifhed by the hand of an affaffin. Milofch Obilitch, one of Lazar's fons-in-law, had been fufpected of being in fecret intelligence with the Turks, and on the eve of the battle, at a banquet given to the Servian chiefs, the Czar offered a goblet to Milofch, and faid that he drank to the fuccefs of his fchemes, even if next day he fhould betray him to the Sultan. Stung by the farcafm, Milofch drained the cup and fwore that he would fhow whether he could prove traitor to his religion and his king. Next morning he went to the Turkifh camp, and being conducted to the tent of the Sultan, knelt before him : then fuddenly rifing he plunged a dagger in his heart, and as he ruſhed out of the tent he was ſeized by the guards and cut to pieces, after a deſperate reſiſtance.

Kóſſovo was the Flodden Field of Servia, but the battle there was more diſaſtrous in its conſequences to her than that of Flodden Field was to Scotland, for it was the firſt ſtep to the abſolute ſupremacy of the Turks.

Bajazet, who ſucceeded Amurath on the Ottoman throne, divided Servia between Stephan, the ſon, and Vuk Brankovitch, the ſon-in-law of Lazar, both of whom bound themſelves to pay tribute to the Sultan, and furniſh troops for the military ſervice of the Sublime Porte. Brankovitch died of poiſon in 1396, and the chief power in Servia became again veſted in a ſingle chief of the old reigning family, who was allowed by the Turks to retain the title of Kral or Deſpot, although really a vaſſal of the Sultan.

In the 15th century a powerful confederacy was formed under the King of Hungary to roll back the tide of Ottoman conqueſt, and it was joined by the Servians, whoſe ruler then was George Brankovitch. The Turks were compelled to retreat after many obſtinate conflicts, and by the Peace or Treaty of Szegedin (July, 1444) they relinquiſhed their hold of Servia, and reſtored it to its independence. But after the death of Brankovitch internal diſſenſions on the queſtions of the rival pretenſions of the Latin and Greek Churches again opened the door to the admiſſion of the Ottomans. They were invited to occupy the fortreſſes, and ſoon became maſters of the country. During the long war between the Hungarians and the Ottomans, Servia ſuffered terribly. They were cruſhed down by the Turks, who had taken Conſtantinople in 1453, and are deſcribed by a traveller of the 16th century as " poor captives, " none of whom dared to lift up his head."* But Auſtria and the Germans came to the reſcue of

* Ranke's Hiſtory of Servia, chap. 2.

Hungary, and the Servians joined the alliance. The refult was that the Crofs triumphed over the Crefcent, and, owing to the brilliant victories of Prince Eugene, the Peace of Paffarowitz was figned in 1718, by which Servia, or at leaft the northern part of it, was delivered from the Turks, and acknowledged the fupremacy of Auftria. But again the fcene fhifted, and in twenty years the complication of European politics placed Servia once more under the dominion of the Ottoman Porte. It then became to all intents and purpofes a Turkifh province, and until the period of their ultimate deliverance, which I fhall narrate hereafter, the Chriftian inhabitants of Servia, like all the other Rayas in the Ottoman kingdom, became " hewers of wood and "drawers of water " to their infidel mafters. They were domineered over by Turkifh Begs under a Turkifh Pacha, had to render heavy feudal fervices, and pay a poll-tax for every male from the age of feven years. Juftice was adminiftered by Muffulman Kadis, whofe pay came chiefly from the Rayas, that is the Chriftian inhabitants. The Bifhops received their infignia of office from the Sultan, and to maintain their dignity were not backward in fleecing their flocks. The Rayas were excluded from all fhare in the conduct of public affairs, and were in fact treated as Serfs, " as the means where-" with to realize a revenue for the fupport of " the State which had fubjugated them, and of " providing for its foldiery, its officers, and " even for the Court."* No Servian dared to ride into a town on horfeback, and to any Turk, who might demand it, he was bound to render perfonal fervice. If he met a Turk in the road, he was obliged to halt and make way for him, and if he carried arms as a defence againft robbers, he had to conceal them. " To fuffer " injuries was his duty ; to refent them was " deemed a crime worthy of punifhment."

* Ranke, chap. iii.

"The Rayas were confidered a weaponlefs herd,
" whofe duty was obedience and fubjection."

The oppreffion of the Turks naturally produced refiftance, and numbers of the male population of Servia, rather than fubmit to their
extortions, abandoned their homes, and, taking
refuge in the forefts, became outlaws and·
brigands. Thefe are the Haiduks fo often
mentioned in Servian hiftory, who waylaid the
Spahis and other Turks in ambufcades, and
robbed and murdered them whenever they had
the opportunity.

By the Peace or Treaty of Belgrade in 1739,
Belgrade, which had been occupied by Auftria,
was reftored to the Porte, and by Art. 3 of the
Treaty, "His Imperial Majefty cedes to the
" Ottoman Porte the Province of Servia, and
" the limits of the two Empires fhall be the
" Danube and the Save."*

But the time of deliverance came at laft. In

* Wenck. Codex Juris Gentium, vol. 1, p. 316, *et seq.*

1788, Ruffia and Auftria combined in war
againft the Sublime Porte, and the Servians
rendered the two Chriftian Powers active
affiftance. A volunteer corps was formed,
which did good fervice at the fiege of Belgrade
in 1789, and next year carried Krufchewatz by
ftorm. · Servia, in fact, was practically re-con-
quered from the Turks ; but the old jealoufies
between the European Powers on the queftion
of the difmemberment of Turkey and aggran-
dizement of any of them at her expenfe, were
for the moment fatal to her caufe. Peace was
made with Turkey in 1791, and Servia was
given back to the Sultan. The only ftipulation
made in favour of the inhabitants was, that an
amnefty fhould be granted to all who had taken
part in the revolt.

But the inveterate mifgovernment went on
as before, and this was met by difturbance and
partial infurrections. It would take too long
to tell the ftory of the Janiffaries and their

hoftile relations with the Sultan, whofe foldiers they were, but who dreaded them as much as any of the Roman Emperors dreaded their Prætorian guards. Let it fuffice to fay that in Servia as elfewhere they fet the orders from Conftantinople at defiance, and fome of them became mere brigands under chiefs called Dahis, who practifed every kind of outrage againft the Chriftian Rayas.

In 1804 a terrible maffacre of thefe took place. The Dahis fpared neither rank nor age. The firft victim was Prince Stanoï, and every Servian of reputation who could be got at was pitileffly murdered. The inhabitants fled to the mountains, and when the Turks approached the villages they found them tenanted only by old men and children. The cruelties of their oppreffors at laft roufed the people to refiftance, and leaders were found in three brave men, George Pétrovitch, better known afterwards as Kara George or "Black George," Janko

Kalitfch, and Vaffo Tfcharapitch. The Turks were everywhere attacked, and compelled to take refuge in their fortreffes. Black George, who had been a mere peafant, received the chief command, and a long and bloody ftruggle enfued. The Janiffaries held Belgrade, which was attacked by the infurgents, and they found unexpected affiftance in the policy of the Ottoman Porte itfelf. That policy was to cripple the power of thofe formidable foldiers, and the Grand Vizier made ufe of the revolt for the purpofe. Békir, the Pacha of Bofnia, was ordered to interfere, not as the enemy but rather as the friend of the Servians. When he entered the country at the head of 3,000 men, he was received by them with every mark of honour and refpect. The commandant at Belgrade did not dare to difobey the direct orders of the Sultan, and on the fummons of the Bofnian Pacha, the gates of the fortrefs were thrown open. The garrifon in the meantime made its efcape by embarking on the Danube and taking refuge in Orfchova. But here the Servians effected an entrance, and feveral of the moft obnoxious of their enemies were put to the fword. After this Békir declared that all was finifhed, and he affured the Servians that they might return peaceably to their occupations.

But, although tranquillity was thus reftored for a time, the caufes of difcontent lay too deep for cure fo long as the yoke of Ottoman defpotifm preffed upon the necks of the Rayas. The old fyftem remained in force—infult and outrage on the part of the Turks, and humiliation and fuffering on the part of the Servians. Again the flame of revolt againft mifrule was kindled, and encouraged by the fympathy which Ruffia had fhown for her Slavonic brethren in Moldavia and Wallachia on the other fide of the Danube, the Servians invoked the protection of the Ruffian Czar. Their appeal was favourably received, and negotiations for a peaceful fettlement of their grievances were fet on foot, but the Porte was ftaggered by one of their demands, which was that all the fortreffes in Servia fhould be placed in their hands. The Servians, however, were determined at all hazards to fecure thefe important places, and, while the negotiations were ftill pending, Kara George appeared at the head of a body of troops before Karanovitz, and, after an attack which in the firft inftance failed, fucceeded in getting poffeffion of the place. Other fortreffes were taken or furrendered by the Turks, and Servia was now in a ftate of open war againft her oppreffors.

While the war againft Napoleon was raging over the continent of Europe, Turkey, in 1807, joined the fide of France, and declared war againft Ruffia. Servia naturally fided with a Chriftian Power of which a great part of the population is Slavonic, and aided Ruffia as fhe beft could in the ftruggle. In the campaign of 1809–10 Kara

George was hard preffed by the Turks, and they would probably have been victorious had not the opportune arrival of a Ruffian army, which croffed the Danube in Auguft, 1809, changed the face of affairs. The Turks were again compelled to quit their hold of Servia, and fhe was able to deliberate on the courfe of policy which it was moft for her intereft to adopt. Perfect independence in fo fmall a ftate midft the clafhing arms of mighty kingdoms feemed practically impoffible, and Kara George at firft wifhed to place the country under the protectorate of Auftria. But Ruffian influence prevailed, and no definitive ftep was taken before the campaign of 1810 opened. The Ruffian General, Kamenfkoï, addreffed a proclamation to the Servians, in which he called them " brothers of the " Ruffians, children of the fame family and the " fame faith," and they heartily refponded to his appeal. The Turks again entered Servia; the former ftruggle was renewed and lafted until

October in that year, when the Turks, having been worſted in a deſperate conflict near Loſnitza, recroſſed the Drina into Boſnia, and an armiſtice was agreed upon, by which that river was made the frontier line which neither army was to paſs.

Diſſenſions, however, between the Servian chiefs now broke out afreſh, and threatened a diſſolution of the government—but the reſult was that the authority of Kara George became ſtronger than ever, and he was from that time practically King or Deſpot of Servia.

But the little State had not been recogniſed as independent by any of the Great Powers, and ſhe was ſtill in theory the vaſſal of the Ottoman Porte, and in the treaty of peace which was ſigned between Ruſſia and Turkey at Buchareſt in 1812, Servia is mentioned as ſubject and tributary to the Sultan. It was therein ſtipulated that the Servian fortreſſes ſhould be garriſoned by Turkiſh troops, but the internal government of the country was to be left to themſelves on payment of a tribute to the Porte—and promifes were made of fecurity and privileges, which long experience has fhown to be utterly worthlefs when made by Turks to Chriftians under their control.

So long as part of the Ruffian army remained in Servia, the inhabitants might confidently rely upon the ftipulations of the treaty being obferved, but Ruffia had now to ftruggle for her own exiftence againft French aggreffion, and all her forces were withdrawn to the north. The Ruffian regiment quartered at Belgrade quitted the country, and Servia was left alone to be trampled under the heel of her hereditary oppreffors.

The inhabitants were ordered to deliver up not only their fortreffes, but their arms; and on their refufal, Turkifh troops began to affemble on the Servian frontier. No longer deterred by fear of Ruffia, whofe power they thought had received a fatal blow at the battle of Lutzen, the Ottoman Porte once more recommenced a Servian war. Never were the fortunes of Servia darker than during this campaign. The Turks victorioufly advanced, and at laft when they croffed the Morawa river, Kara George, having firft buried his treafure, fled acrofs the Danube, and took refuge in Auftrian territory, where he was foon followed by the Servian Senators. The whole country was now defencelefs, and the Turks took poffeffion of Belgrade without refiftance.

There was, however, one man whofe fortitude did not fail him in this hour of extremeft peril. This was Milofch Obrenovich, who in early youth had herded fwine in the Servian forefts. He had become a Voivode, but did not, like the other Voivodes, abandon Servia. When urged to fly he nobly faid, " No ! whatever may be " the fate of my fellow-countrymen shall be " mine alfo." At firft the Turks tried the policy of conciliation, and induced Milofch, who had neither the means nor the power to make an effectual refiftance, to fubmit to their authority.

He and other chiefs became reconciled to the Porte, and he received from it a confirmation of his dignity as Grand Knes of Rudnik.

But, as Ranke fays, the Turks having recovered poffeffion of the country by hoftile invafion, governed as they thought fit. In other words, their rule was as oppreffive as ever, and taking advantage of a partial attempt at infur-rection, in the autumn of 1814, Soliman Pacha caufed 150 of thofe who had been engaged in it to be carried to Belgrade and there beheaded. Others were impaled alive. Some were bound hand and foot, and fufpended by the extremities, with heavy ftones hung from the middle of their bodies. Some were flogged to death ; others roafted alive on fpits. In anfwer to all remonftrances, the Pacha faid that he was ftill far from acting up to his inftructions from

44

the Porte, that in fact he was sparing the country! These atrocities changed the conduct of Milosch. He felt that his own life was no longer safe, and the miseries of his countrymen were at their full. They were ready to hazard everything rather than endure the continued curse of Turkish tyranny, and after a short period of secret organisation, Milosch came forward as their leader and hoisted the standard of insurrection.

On Palm Sunday 1815 he appeared in the midst of an assembly at Zrnutscha, fully armed and with the banner of a Voivode in his hand, crying out: "Here am I! and now war against "the Turks is begun!" The revolt spread rapidly, and was as rapidly successful. In general the Turks made a poor resistance, and hastily retreated from the open ground, sheltering themselves in their fortifications. Several of these were taken or abandoned, and the strong entrenchment of Poscherawatz was carried after a fierce ftruggle. The Bofnian Pacha, Ali, who came to the affiftance of his countrymen, was defeated by Milofch and taken prifoner. But notwithftanding thefe fucceffes, the fate of Servia hung trembling in the balance. The principal fortreffes were ftill held by the Turks, and two formidable Turkifh armies, were on the march to crufh the infurrection, when happily peaceful counfels prevailed at Conftantinople and the war ended without further bloodfhed.

Deputies from Servia appeared at the Congrefs of Vienna in 1815, but little attention was paid to their complaints and earneft prayers for recognition and help. But the two Turkifh armies that were advancing againft Servia halted on their march, owing to orders from Conftantinople, and negotiations were opened with a view to peace. Milofch ventured to truft himfelf in the Turkifh lines, but when he found one of the demands was that the Servian population fhould not be allowed to retain their arms, he inflexibly refufed, and left the camp. Soon afterwards, however, the commander of the Turkifh army on the Bofnian frontier, withdrew the obnoxious ftipulation, faying, "only "be fubmiffive to the Grand Signor, and you "may carry as many piftols in your belts as "you pleafe—cannon even, for what I care!" The refult was that the Servians allowed the Turks to occupy Belgrade, and there Milofch, in a folemn conference, on being afked by the Pacha, "Are ye Servians fubject to the Grand "Signor?" anfwered "We are fubject to him." The queftion and anfwer were repeated thrice.

The fortreffes of Servia were now garrifoned by the Turks with the confent of the inhabitants, and an Embaffy was fent to Conftantinople to regulate the terms on which the country was in future to be governed. In the meantime "the "haughty infolence of the Ottomans difplayed "itfelf in the rudeft and moft offenfive conduct."*

* Ranke, Hift. of Servia, chap. xviii.

But diffenfions broke out again amongft the Servian chiefs themfelves. They were jealous of the authority of Milofch, and tried to thwart his influence. Kara George had returned to Servia, and a league called the Hetaira (not confined to Servia alone), was formed, the members of which fwore to fight with the enemies of their country until they were annihilated. Kara George placed himfelf at the head of this league, and invited Milofch to join and renew the ftruggle for independence. But Milofch refufed to do this, and denounced Kara George to the Pacha, who told him to bring him his head. Milofch iffued his orders, or at all events indicated where Kara George was to be found, and he was bafely murdered while he was afleep. This great crime left Milofch without any dangerous rival, and in November 1817 he was acknowledged by the Servians Supreme *Knes* or Ruler of the whole of Servia.

Matters remained in an unfettled ftate as

regards the relations of Servia to the Ottoman Porte until 1820, when a Firman 'was fent from Conftantinople fpecifying the conceffions which the Sultan had refolved to grant. The authority of the Muffulmans was to be reftricted to the fortreffes, and Milofch was recognifed as the Grand Knes of Servia. A fixed tribute was alfo fubftituted for the former varying amount. But there were other conditions which were ftrongly unpalatable to the Servians. They were to remain "Imperial Rayas" as their forefathers had been, they were to provide for the Turkifh armies whenever they might happen to pafs through the country, and they were required formally to promife that they would never again demand anything more from the Grand Seigneur. They therefore refufed to accept the terms, and an embaffy was sent to Conftantinople to prefent the demands which would fatisfy the nation. The deputies however when they reached the capital were put under arreft, and, that he might not be compromifed by any agreement they might make while under durefs Milofch withdrew his credentials from them.

The Greek revolution now broke out and materially changed the attitude of the Great Powers, and efpecially of Ruffia, towards the Ottoman Porte and her vaffal ftates. Ruffia determined to exact a literal fulfilment of the Treaty of Buchareft, which in fome refpects had remained in abeyance for feveral years. The Sultan, terrified at the afpect of affairs, and threatened by the three Great Powers, England, France and Ruffia, did not dare to refift, and having firft fet at liberty the Servian deputies who had been ftill detained at Conftantinople, he promifed to enter into negotiations with the Servian people, for fecuring to it all the privi·· leges conceded by the Treaty of Buchareft. The refult was that, by the Convention of Ackerman in October, 1826, Servia was erected into a Principality tributary to the Porte, but with an independent internal adminiſtration.

But the Ottoman Porte could only be truſted ſo far as it was coerced by fear, and it began to play its old game of faſt and looſe. In a *hatti-ſheriff* iſſued in December, 1827, the Sultan made the ominous declaration that he had yielded to the demands of the Servians only from the preſſure of circumſtances, and that he had entered into the Convention of Ackerman only to gain the time neceſſary to prepare for war. And war began in earneſt between Ruſſia and the Porte, and was continued until the victorious flag of Ruſſia was carried across the Balkan, when, to avert the capture of Conſtantinople, the Ottoman Porte gave way, and conſented to the terms impoſed upon her. She agreed to recogniſe Greece as an independent kingdom, and by the Treaty of Adrianople in 1829, the Sultan pledged himſelf to perform the ſtipulations of the Conference of Ackerman with reference to

E 2

Servia " without the leaſt delay, and with· the
" moſt conſcientious exactneſs."

In conformity with that Treaty, the Porte
iſſued on the 1ſt of October, 1829, a *hatti-
ſheriff* which provided amongſt other things
that the Servians " might freely exerciſe in their
" country their mode of worſhip, and follow
" their own religion ; that the adminiſtration
" of the internal affairs of their country might
" be under their own authority, and that the dif-
" ferent kinds of taxes, revenues, and capitation
" duties might be all conſolidated and fixed into
" one sum." Moreover, the important ſtipula-
tion was added, that " the Muſſulmans or Turks,
" except those who are to guard the caſtles,
" ſhould be prohibited to reſide in Servia." *

And in 1830 a Firman was granted by the

* See Hertſlet's Map of Europe by Treaty, 1814–1875, vol. ii.
p. 833. When Lord Ponſonby, on behalf of Great Britain, ſug-
geſted certain modifications, the Sultan refuſed to recogniſe any
right in Great Britain to interfere in the affairs of Servia,
but admitted the right of Ruſſia under her treaties with the
Porte.

Sultan, by which he formally recognifed Milofch Obrenovich as " Prince of Servia," and decreed that the dignity fhould be hereditary in his family. He alfo folemnly promifed that the Sublime Porte would not interfere, in any manner whatever, either in the internal adminiftration or in the affairs of the country ; and that it fhould not be allowed to " exact a fingle *para* " beyond the ufual tribute." * Another concef- fion was that, " with the exception of the Im- " perial fortreffes which anciently exifted in " Servia, all thofe that have been erected lately " fhall be demolifhed." But it was ftipulated that when the dignity of Prince of Servia became vacant, the new Prince fhould pay the sum of 100,000 piaftres when he received from the Sub- lime Porte " the noble *Berat* of inveftiture." This affertion of fovereignty was more explicitly made in a fubfequent Firman granted in 1833, one of the articles of which provided that " neither you

* Ibid. p. 843.

" (the Prince) nor the Servian nation fhall ever act
" in any manner whatever contrary to the duties
" of faithful fubjects, nor contrary to the fub-
" miffion which you owe to the Sublime Porte."*

The recognition of Milofch as Prince of
Servia was in accordance with a folemn refolu-
tion of the *Skoupfchina*, or General Affembly,
and the wifh of the whole Servian nation. He
thus became the undifputed Ruler of Servia, and
the founder of a new dynafty, although he could
neither read nor write!

His government was fevere and harfh, and
practically abfolute, and he had to put down
more than one attempt at infurrection againft his
authority. "He exercifed," fays Ranke, "the
" power of life and death as defpotically and as
" unfcrupuloufly as any Turkifh Pacha." But
he had the good fenfe to fee that tyranny only
aggravates difcontent, and in 1835 he granted

* See Hertflet's Map of Europe by Treaty, 1814–1875, vol. ii.
p. 933.

a Conftitutional Charter to Servia, which, under the name of the Servian Code, for the time fatisfied the people.

Still, however, Milofch governed in an arbitrary manner, and many acts of injuftice, and even cruelty, are recorded of him, which made him very unpopular. "At laft," fays Ranke, "as the outrages of which the Knes was "accufed were flagrant and undeniable," an urgent warning was given by the Court of St. Peterfburg to Milofch to act with more juftice and humanity. Servian deputies alfo went to Conftantinople, and laid their grievances before the Sultan, and the refult was that a new Conftitutional Charter was framed, limiting the power of Milofch, and increafing the power of the Senate, whofe members, feventeen in number, were, however, to be appointed by the Prince for life. This was in 1839. Milofch met the change with fullen oppofition; and amongft the peafantry, with whom he was more popular than in the towns, he foftered a fpirit of refiftance to the new charter, which broke out in fome places into violence. He was ftrongly oppofed by many of the chiefs, and one of them, named *Wutfchitfk*, who was appointed to the military command againft the infurgents, having compelled a large body of them to furrender, took Milofch's brother Jovan prifoner while he was endeavouring to collect a frefh band of adherents to fupport, as he faid, the authority of his brother the Prince. The Senate, therefore, determined to depofe Milofch, and his refidence at Belgrade having been furrounded with troops, he, on the 13th of June, 1839, figned a formal inftrument of abdication in favour of his eldeft fon Milan. But Milan at the time was in bad health, and he foon afterwards died, without, it is faid, having ever known that he was Prince of Servia.

Michael, his younger brother, was alive, but his name was not in the line of fucceffion which had been guaranteed by the Porte. The Senate, therefore, determined to aſk the Sultan to ſanction Michael's appointment to the vacant throne, and the requeſt was granted.

The rule of Michael was a diſturbed one, and he had to contend againſt a ſtrong oppoſition, ſupported by the partiſans of Miloſch. The Turks took advantage of the difficulty, and became more preſſing in obnoxious demands. At laſt, hearing that a *Skoupſchina* was about to be held in order to compel him to change his adminiſtration, Michael took the field, and advanced againſt the malcontents, who were already in arms, under the command of *Wutſchitſk*. A parley was agreed upon, but Michael refuſed to conſent to the conditions which were offered. He was deſerted by his ſoldiers, and at laſt abandoned Servia, and took refuge acroſs the Auſtrian frontier, while *Wutſhitcſk* entered Belgrade in triumph, and, ſtyling himſelf " Leader of the " Nation," aſſumed the chief authority.

57

A Provifional Government was formed, and a *Skoupfchina* fummoned in September, 1842, to determine who fhould be Ruler of Servia. With one voice they declared that they would not have Michael, and with equal unanimity they declared in favour of Alexander Kara Georgevich, the fon of their former favourite leader Kara George, or Black George. Their choice was confirmed by the Porte, but Ruffia refufed to acknowledge the change of dynafty—at all events, not unlefs a new election took place, for fhe alleged that the former one was made in hafte and tumult. Accordingly, in 1843, another *Skoupfchina* was affembled, and again Kara Georgevich was unanimoufly chofen Prince of Servia.

He received the *Berat* of inveftiture from the Sultan, and proved himfelf a wife and able ruler. During his fway many internal improvements were made, not the leaft important of which were good roads. Education was carefully attended to, and military fchools, and fchools of commerce and agriculture, were eftablifhed.

When the quarrel took place between Ruffia and the Porte in 1853, which led to the Crimean War, Georgevich obferved a ftrict neutrality, and would not yield to the natural defire of the Servians to feize the opportunity of fhaking themfelves entirely free from Turkifh fovereignty. For this fidelity to the Ottoman Porte he received a Firman confirming the liberties and privileges of the Servian people.

By the 28th article of the Treaty of Paris, 1856, it was provided : " The Principality of " Servia fhall continue to hold of the Sublime " Porte, in conformity with the Imperial Hats " which fix and determine its rights and immu- " nities, placed henceforward under the collective " guarantee of the contracting Powers. In confe- " quence the faid Principality fhall preferve its " independent and national adminiftration, as

" well as full liberty of worfhip, of legiflation, of
" commerce, and of navigation."

In 1857, a confpiracy was formed againft
Georgevich by the partifans of the depofed
Milofch. The Prefidents of the Senate and of
the Court of Appeal were accomplices, and they
were arrefted and condemned to death ; but at
the inftance of the Porte, fupported by the
remonftrances of the confuls of France and
Ruffia at Belgrade, they were reprieved. The
Skoupfchina, however, called on Georgevich to
abdicate, and he quitted Servia. He was then
(December, 1857) declared depofed, and Milofch
was recalled, and reftored to the dignity of Prince
of Servia. He continued to reign until his
death in September, 1860, when he was fucceeded by his fon, Michael Obrenovich III.

In 1862, the Turks bombarded Belgrade to
avenge a quarrel between a Turkifh foldier and
a Servian, who was killed by the Turk. A
long diplomatic ftruggle followed, England and

Auftria taking part with Turkey, and France, Ruffia, and Pruffia fiding with Servia. The refult was that Turkey agreed to evacuate the Servian fortreffes.

Prince Michael proved himfelf an energetic ruler. He armed the nation, eftablifhing an arfenal, and procuring mufkets from Ruffia. But in June, 1868, he was affaffinated at Belgrade, while he was walking in a park. He was met by three members of the Radovanitch family — a father and two fons — the former of whom had for fome offence been punifhed with imprifonment. They fired their piftols at the Prince, and he fell mortally wounded. At the fame time two ladies, his coufins, with whom he was walking, were attacked by the affaffins and murdered. A Provifional Government was immediately formed ; the regicides were committed for trial, and ten other perfons were arrefted on the charge of being implicated in a confpiracy to place Prince Kara Georgevich on the throne. Prince Milan Obrenovich, the fon of the former ruler, was elected to fill the vacant throne, and as he was then a minor, a Council of Regency was formed to hold office until he came of age. At the fame time the *Skoupfchina* paffed a law by which Prince Kara Georgevich and his defcendants were declared incapable of wearing the Servian Crown.

When the news of the affaffination of Prince Michael and the formation of a Provifional Government reached Conftantinople, the Ottoman Porte immediately communicated to the Provifional Government its defire that the refult of the election of a Prince of Servia, " which " ought to be fubmitted for the fanction of the " Sultan," fhould be in accordance with the legitimate needs of the country, and that the Servian nation fhould exercife its electoral rights with all the liberty compatible with order and due regard to law. But in a note addreffed to the Great Powers in June, 1868, by Fuad

Pacha, he faid that while the Sublime Porte left to the Servian people its free choice of a new Prince, it was refolved to fanction only the election of one who was a native of Servia (*originaire du pays*).

The Turks had ftill continued to garrifon Belgrade, Semendria, and five other fortreffes; but now they have abfolutely quitted the foil of Servia, and the folitary fymbol of titular fovereignty on the part of the Ottoman Porte is a green flag that floats on the ramparts of Belgrade. *

The national religion of Servia is that of the Greek church. The Archbifhop and Bifhops acknowledge the primacy of the Patriarch of Conftantinople, " but know nothing, and ac-" knowledge nothing of a fupremacy in that " Patriarch."† Perfect toleration of Chriftian

---

* Belgrade is properly Beo-grad, " the white town."

† Servia and the Servians, by Rev. W. Denton, London 1862, p. 86.

worſhip was ſecured by a law of September, 1853, and although there is no expreſs ſanction of the Jewiſh religion, a ſynagogue exiſts at Belgrade, which the Jews frequent without hindrance or moleſtation. Accórding to the cenſus of 1866, there were in Servia 3409 Roman Catholics; 352 Proteſtants, and 4965 Mahometans.

The Conſtitution of Servia conſiſts of the Prince, aſſiſted by a council of ſeven miniſters, a ſenate, and a *Skoupſchina,** or Houſe of Repreſentatives. The ſenate conſiſts of 17 members, nominated by the Prince, who ſit *en permanence*— one for each of the 17 Departments into which the Principality is divided. The *Skoupſchina* is compoſed of 134 deputies, of whom 33 are nominated by the Government and 101 choſen by the electors, at the rate of one deputy for every 2000 electors. The electors are the male inhabitants above the age of 21 years, paying direct taxes, and not being domeſtic ſervants or gipſies.

* *Skoupſchina* is derived from the Slavonic verb *ſkoupiti,* to aſſemble.

As regards its internal adminiftration, Servia is divided into 17 departments, 60 fub-departments, and 1059 *communes*. Thefe communes, which include villages and hamlets, are governed by municipal officers called *kmètes*, who are affifted in the difcharge of fome of their functions by village councils, called *fkoupe*, compofed of the head men of the village. " Every Sunday the heads of the village families meet to " form the *fkoupe*. The affembly is held in the " open air, and lafts four or five hours. In the " centre fits the *kmète*, furrounded by the chief " men, and with their aid and advice he fettles " difputes, difcuffes the wants of each village, " and makes known the decrees of the Govern- " ment." Such, at leaft, was the parochial fyftem in Servia a few years ago ; but I am not fure that it has not been modified by recent legiflation.

The foil of Servia is fertile and productive, but three-fourths of its furface are uncultivated.

The people are averfe to labour, either as culti-- vators or artizans, and the peafants, rather than work themfelves, employ for the conftruction of their cottages itinerant mafons and carpenters, who flock yearly in fwarms from the adjacent provinces of Albania and Macedonia.* The chief grain is maize, but the country produces hemp, flax, tobacco, and cotton.

The laft Confular Report in Servia which has been publifhed, fo far as I am aware, is dated March, 1872. The population is there ftated to be 1,100,000 fouls.† As in all the other Danubian provinces, the roads are bad ; indeed, they are hardly paffable except when a hard froft has fet in. Servia has as yet no railways.

The exports of the Principality are corn (which conflitutes generally three per cent. of the whole), wool (averaging £60,000 a year),

* Confular Report on Servia for 1872.

† But according to the cenfus of 1866 the population was 1,216,346, of whom 24,607 were gipfies, and 2,509 German fettlers.

tallow, fpirits, made from the plum, which go into Auftria to be rectified, ftaves for cafks, of which £13,000 are exported yearly; and laft, but not leaft, *pigs*, for the pig trade amounts to nearly one-half of the whole value of the exports of the Principality. They find their way chiefly into Hungary, where they are melted down for their fat. Salt cannot properly be included amongft the exports, although a very large quantity paffes the frontier outwards; for it is not produced in Servia, but paffes through it from Wallachia into Auftria, and is in fact chiefly fmuggled. There is a copper mine at Maidanpek, belonging to an Englifh company, which produces about £13,000 of copper yearly, and is capable of confiderable increafe.

As regards imports, the Confular Report fays the trade in cotton goods and yarns has very largely increafed of late years. In 1864, it was only £2,000, but in 1871-2 it had reached to £30,000 in one year.

HITHERTO we have been fpeaking of the Principality of Free Servia, but there is a diftrict due fouth of it which is properly Stara Servia, or Old Servia, although called by the Turks Arnaoutluk, and confidered part of northern Albania, as appears from the various confular reports. This diftrict contains about half a million inhabitants, and its hiftory is curious. " Previous to " 1389 it was the moft flourifhing and favoured " portion of European Serbia ; at prefent, excepting the neighbouring mountains of Al" bania, it is the pooreft and worft ruled part of " Turkey in Europe."* The year 1389 is the date of the battle of Kóffovo, when the Servians were conquered by the Turks. Old Servia fol-

* Travels in the Slavonic Provinces of Turkey in Europe, by Muir Mackenzie and Irby, p. 246.

lowed the fortunes of (what is now) Free Servia
until the latter part of the feventeenth century,
when Auftria took up arms to repel Turkifh
invafion, and called upon the Servians to affift
her in the ftruggle. They obeyed the call, and
the Auftrians advanced as far fouth as Kóffovo
Polié, or the Plain of Kóffovo, when they were
driven back and compelled to abandon the
country fouth of the Danube. As the effect of
this retreat was to leave Servia at the mercy of
the Turks, the German emperor offered an
afylum in his own dominions north of the
Danube to as many of the inhabitants of Old
Servia as chofe to emigrate. The confequence
was that in 1690, 37,000 families, under the
guidance of their patriarch Arfenius Tfrnoïevitch,
quitted Old Servia and fettled themfelves along
the frontier north of the Danube and the Save.
Here they have remained, and form a great part of
the Slavonic population that guards the military
frontier of Auftria. Old Servia had thus become

almoft denuded of her Chriftian inhabitants, and their place was gradually filled by Albanians, or, as the Turks call them, Arnaouts, from the neighbouring mountains on the weft and fouth. Thefe Albanians were for the moft part Chriftians of the Latin Church; but after they had fettled in Old Servia they gradually adopted the Muffulman creed, and at the prefent time there are only a few Roman Catholic Albanians in the diftrict. The defcendants of the Muffulman converts feem, however, to have little fympathy with the other Turks. "Their antagonifm to "the authority of the Porte is quite as marked "as their arrogance to the Chriftians. 'Fear "'God little,' fay the Arnaouts of Ipek [the "principal town in Old Servia], 'and as for the "'Sultan, do not know that he lives.'"*

But there is ftill left in the diftrict a remnant of the families of Old Servia who are Chriftians—

* Travels in the Slavonic Provinces of Turkey in Europe, p. 253, by Muir Mackenzie and Irby.

a fmall minority in the midft of Muffulmans— and they have an evil time of it. Leaving the towns to the Mahometans, they dwell chiefly in villages and the country. They are heavily taxed, and we are told by eye-witneffes that " the condition of the country is bad enough to " reduce to defpair all its inhabitants, excepting, " of courfe, thofe evil men who thrive on it." It is no wonder that they look with longing eyes to their brethren in the Principality of Free Servia that adjoins them on the north ; but it is faid that the Government there difcourages emigration from Old Servia, becaufe this would tend to abandon the anceftral home of the race wholly to Mahometans, and thus what I fuppofe the Free Servians would call a feeling of patriotifm is indulged in at the expenfe of the fufferings of their unfortunate fellow-Chriftians, and in reality fellow-countrymen.

BOSNIA.

III.

BOSNIA.

BOSNIA takes its name from Bosna, a tribu-tary of the Save which flows into the Danube at Belgrade.

It is bounded on the north by the Save, which feparates it from Slavonia, and on the eaſt by the Drina, which is the frontier line between Boſnia and Servia: on the weſt by Dalmatia, and on the fouth by Montenegro and Albania.

The name of Boſnia firſt emerges in the feventh century in the midſt of the irruption of the Serbs into the countries south of the Danube, as I have already mentioned. So far as the obſcure hiſtory of thoſe times can be truſted the preſent Boſnia ſeems to have been

75

occupied by Croats in the eighth century, and
to have formed part of the poffeffions of the
Archbifhopric of Spalato.* It fluctuated, however, for many years under Croatian and Servian
dominion, but in the eleventh century we find
a Ban of Bofnia as one of the feven Electors
with whom refted the election of a king of
Croatia.† After the extinction of that dynafty,
the King of Hungary in 1102 affumed the
crown of Dalmatia and Croatia, and he alfo
called himfelf King of Rama, which name
properly belonged to the prefent diftrict of
Herzegovina, and was derived from the river

---

* See Von Thoemmel, Befchreibung des Vilayet Bofnien,
Wien, 1865.

† The word Croats is a corruption of Chrobates, a Slavonic
tribe who fpread themfelves over Illyricum and Dalmatia. In
courfe of time their different hordes roamed northwards, and
peopled the countries now known as Croatia and Slavonia.
Bofnia was at firft included in the general name of Croatia under
the Greek Empire. "The Chrobatians, or Croats, who now
"attend the motions of an Auftrian army, are the defcendants
"of a mighty people, the conquerors and fovereigns of Dal-
"matia."—Gibbon, Decline and Fall, chap. 55.

Rama which flows in it. But it was ufed in-
differently for Bofnia, and we find in old
charters the expreffion *Rex Rhamæ seu
Bofniæ.* For feveral centuries Bofnia remained
a Banat under the dominion of Hungary, and
one of the Bans named Kulin in the twelfth
century defcribed himfelf as *Fiduciarius Regni
Hungariæ.* He is faid to have been the firft
who coined money in Bofnia, and introduced
foreign artificers into the territory. His name
is ftill remembered among the people as mark-
ing the era of a diftant golden age.* The
Banat lafted until the fourteenth century, when
Stephan Turtko in 1376 exchanged the title of
Ban for that of King, and was folemnly crowned
in the monaftery of Milofevo near Priepolje.

At the difaftrous battle of Kóffovo in 1389,

* From an article on Bofnia by Mifs Irby, who is one of the
two accomplifhed authoreffes of Travels in Slavonia, and who,
during the laft few years, has refided much at Serajevo, the
capital of Bofnia, in purfuance of a fcheme for training native
fchoolmiftreffes.

when the Servian power was fhattered by the
Turks, 20,coo Bofnians fought fide by fide
with their Slavonic brethren, and their leader
was able after the defeat to make good his return
to Bofnia at the head of his troops, who victorioufly repelled the Turks when they preffed
forward in purfuit.

The hiftory of the next feventy years is a
confufed record of war and inteftine troubles
under native Bans and Kings, until the Sultan
Mohammed II. in the fifteenth century invaded
Bofnia with an overwhelming force and reduced
it to fubjection, making it tributary to the Porte.
And when the King of Bofnia attempted foon
afterwards to free himfelf from the yoke and
refufed to pay the ftipulated tribute, the Sultan
again in 1463 invaded the country, and taking
fortrefs after fortrefs became undifputed mafter
of Bofnia. The king and many of the nobility,
Voivodes and others, were put to death, 30,000
of the youth were drafted into the ranks of the

Janiffaries, and a large number of the inhabitants reduced to slavery. A Turkifh Vizier was appointed to adminifter the government, and he took up his refidence at Bofna Serai, now generally called Serajevo.

But the Kings of Hungary had never given up their pretenfion to be confidered lords of Bofnia, and almoft immediately after the Sultan had quitted the country which he had fo cruelly ravaged, Mathias Corvinus, King of Hungary, marched into Bofnia and made himfelf mafter of many of the towns and fortreffes in fpite of the ftrong oppofition of the Turks.

From this time forward for upwards of fixty years Bofnia was divided between the two contending powers of Hungary and the Ottoman Porte, and was the fcene of conftant ftruggles between the hoftile camps. But the Crefcent prevailed againft the Crofs, for the King of Hungary was too weak to defend the extremities of his kingdom. In the year 1527, the whole of Bofnia had fallen into the hands of the Turks, and as part of their dominion it has remained from that time to the prefent day. Not however without frequent ftruggles for independence, the laft of which occurred in 1849–51.

The Muffulmans of Bofnia were ftrongly oppofed to the introduction of the *Tanzimatu*, the celebrated code of reforms promulgated by the Sultan Abdul Medjid; and when in 1849 the Porte attempted to force it on the province, it was refifted. A confpiracy of Muffulman chiefs was formed, whofe place of rendezvous was the Kraina,* which has generally been the theatre of infurrectionary movements in Bofnia. To reprefs this, one of the moft diftinguifhed Turkifh generals, Omer Pacha, who was by birth an Auftro-Servian and a convert to the faith of Iflam, was fent into the country at the head of a powerful force, but it was not until after a long and obftinate refiftance that he was

---

* I believe the meaning of Kraina is " frontier."

able in 1851 to accomplifh his object. The reforms were no doubt in the main favourable to the Chriftians, but one ftipulation was moft obnoxious to them. They were ordered to give up their arms and forbidden to wear them, although afterwards the Sultan granted particular exceptions in favour of individuals when permiffion was afked through the prietts or foreign confuls.

One remarkable effect of the conqueft of Bofnia by the Turks was, that a confiderable part of the population embraced the Muffulman religion. We muft never forget this when fpeaking, not only of the Bofnians, but alfo of other Muffulmans in Turkey in Europe. They are not Ofmanlis—not of the fame race as thofe fierce Orientals who croffed the Bofphorus, and made fubject to their fway fome of the faireft regions of the earth. The confequence is that they have always been diftinguifhed by a fpirit of oppofition to the central authority of Conftan- ·

tinople, and some writers who have had opportunities, by refidence in Bofnia, of clofely obferving the temper of the people, are of opinion that the Bofnian Muffulmans would, in cafe Bofnia became independent of the Porte, have little difficulty in changing their religion, and embracing the Chriftian creed of their forefathers. I think, however, that this is more than doubtful—for hitherto they have been diftinguifhed by a very fanatical hatred of the Rayas, and are by them more hated than the Ofmanli Turks.

The old Bofnian nobility, whofe forefathers became Muffulmans, have been metamorphofed into Begs and Agas. But their power is gone, and their caftles are crumbling into decay. They are excluded from official pofts by the jealoufy of the Ottoman Porte, and being too proud to engage in induftrial purfuits, they live poor and with little influence. Their old rank of Spahis, or feudal military chiefs, has been abolifhed, and the tithe they formerly received from the peafants is paid into the Government Treafury. They are defcribed as ignorant, corrupt, indolent, and wholly incapable of organization or combined action.

The Muffulman population fills the towns, while the Chriftian Rayas chiefly occupy the villages, which are fcattered far apart.

In ancient times HERZEGOVINA formed part of Illyricum, and was included in the Roman province of Dalmatia. Under the old Servian dominion, the eaftern part of it, which was called Humska, was a Zupania; but after the battle of Kóffovo and the difmemberment of Servia, the Zupans of Humfka, who were the defcendants of Stephan Nemandia, quarrelled amongft themfelves for the chief rule, and Stephan IV., the Ban of Bofnia, taking advantage of their diffenfions, incorporated the diftrict with his own dominions. This was in 1334. For fifty-five years it remained part of Bofnia, but in 1389 Turtko I., who was then King of Bofnia, granted it as a fief to one of the Voivodes, Vlatko Hranié, who, as well as his fon and fucceffor Sandlaj, ftood firmly by their liege lord, the ruler of Bofnia, in his contefts with the Turks, and contributed materially to his fuccefsful refiftance. After the death of Sandlaj in 1435, Vlatko's nephew, Stephan Kofaca, fucceeded him, and he extended the limits of his territory by abforbing part of the lands of Bofnia proper, and adding the old Zupania of Rafcia. At laft he threw off his allegiance to the King of Bofnia, and acknowledged himfelf the vaffal of the German Emperor, Frederick IV.

In confequence of this, Frederick beftowed upon him the title of Herzog, or Duke, from which the province derives its prefent name.

Duke Stephan was an ambitious ruler, bent on aggrandizing his own domain ; but he was fhort-fighted enough to ftand aloof and render no affiftance to the King of Bofnia when the Turks burſt into the country in 1463, and reduced it to ſubjection.

Herzegovina ſoon followed the fate of Boſnia, and became tributary to the Porte. Stephan placed in its hands as a hoſtage his youngeſt ſon, who became a Muſſulman, and married one of the daughters of the Sultan. He died in 1466, and ſoon afterwards Herzegovina became a Turkiſh province—in fact, nothing more than a Sandjak of the Vilayet of Boſnia, and as ſuch it has remained to the preſent day.* Sir Gardner Wilkinſon ſays :—" The miſeries endured by the " people when conquered by the Turks . . and " the perſecutions that led to the flight of " thouſands of Slavonian Chriſtians are ſcarcely " known, or ceaſe to preſent the picture of woe " that for years afflicted the unhappy countries " (Boſnia and Herzegovina)." †

* Von Thoemmel, Beſchreibung des Vilayet Boſnien.

† Dalmatia and Montenegro, vol. ii. p. 97. The chief town in Herzegovina is Mostar, on the banks of the Narenta. It was once a Roman Municipium, called Mandertium or Matrix.

There are in Bosnia about 1800 Turkish mosques, but many of these are mere wooden buildings.

The population of the whole country, including Herzegovina, according to the latest official reports, is 1,216,846, thus divided :—

Bosnian Muffulmans . . .	442,050
Christians of the Greek Church . .	576,756
Roman Catholics . .	185,503
Jews	3,000
Gipfies . .	9.537
	1,216,846

Besides these there are about 5000 Austrian subjects, and a few hundreds of Turkish officials.

The Roman Catholic population has for centuries acknowledged as its immediate superior authority in matters of religion the Provincial Order of Minorites of St. Francis of Affifi, to which it was made subject by the Pope Leo X. in 1517.* Herzegovina, however, in 1852, withdrew itself from their authority. There still

* Von Thoemmel, Befchreibung des Vilayet Bofnien.

exifts a Firman by which the Sultan Mahomet, in 1463, granted fpecial privileges to the Bofnian monks, and forbade them to be molefted or dif-turbed. But this could not prevent the ravages of war and diforder, and of the thirty old monafteries which once exifted in Bofnia, it is faid that in 1860 only three remained. But fince then the number has been increafed, and three ftately monafteries have been built, one in Herzegovina, and the others in Bofnia Proper.

The Greek Church in Bofnia ufes a Slavonic Liturgy, and the members of the Communion call their religion the Pravoflav, which is the fame as that of the Ruffians; but they are forced againft their will to fubmit to the jurif-diction of the Greek Patriarch at Conftantinople.

The Jews live chiefly in the capital, Serajevo (the old Bofna Serai), and are there a profperous community. But they are met with alfo in fome of the other provincial towns, fuch as Moftar (the capital of Herzegovina) and Travnik.

The gipfies in Bofnia are like all gipfies in the reft of the world, and their occupation is defcribed as " fmith-work, begging, and thiev- " ing." *

While on the fubject of religion in Bofnia, I may mention that there exifted there for feveral centuries a Proteftant fect known by the name of Paterenes or Bogomilen, faid to have been founded by an Armenian named Bafil in the reign of the Emperor Alexius Comnenus. The origin of the name Paterenes is uncertain, fome deriving it from *patior*, which means " fuffering," —and this would not inaptly defcribe the hiftory of their perfecutions. They denied the fove- reignty of the Pope, the power of the priefts, the efficacy of prayers for the dead, and the exiftence of purgatory. In many refpects their pofition and doctrine remind us of the Albi- genfes. Pope Innocent III., who made himfelf confpicuous by his perfecuting zeal againft

* Von Thoemmel, p. 109.

heretics, called upon the King of Hungary, who then was Suzerain of Bofnia, to expel all the Paterenes from the territory ; but Kulin, the Ban of Bofnia, evaded the order, and continued to encourage the Paterenes until his death at the end of the 12th century. Succeeding Popes fulminated their anathemas againft the increafing fect, but they continued to flourifh, not without many viciffitudes of fortune, until the reign of Stephan, King of Bofnia, who, in 1449, ordered all the Paterenes to leave Bofnia Proper, which was under his immediate fway, and 40,000 of them took refuge in Herzegovina. "From "that period little is known about them in thofe "parts of Europe." *

Bofnia Proper, as diftinguifhed from Herzegovina, is a rugged mountainous country full of magnificent forefts. The climate of Herzegovina is much milder, efpecially in the fouth, and in its

* Dalmatia and Montenegro, by Sir G. Wilkinfon, vol. ii. p. 113.

lower valleys the vine and the olive flourish abundantly. There are also mulberries, figs, rice, and tobacco.* " The soil of Bosnia teems " with various and valuable minerals, her hills " abound in splendid forests, her well-watered " plains are fertile and productive ; her race, " under culture, proves exceptionally gifted."†
But what is the condition of the people ?

" La Bosnie est de toutes les provinces " turques celle où la civilisation a fait le moins " de progrès."‡ Miss Irby, who has long resided in Bosnia, describes it as " the most barbarous of " the provinces of Turkey in Europe. . . . . The " mass of the people are ground to the dust under " the present *régime*. . . . . There is no develop- " ment of the immense material resources of the

---

* See La Bosnie considérée dans ses rapports avec l'Empire Ottoman, par Pertusier ; and Von Thoemmel, Beschreibung des Vilayet Bosnien.

† I take this description from Miss Irby's article on Bosnia, before mentioned.

‡ Provinces Danubiennes, par MM. Chopin et Ubicini, p. 239.

"country, no means of employment and occupa-
" tion, which might enable the poor to meet the
" ever increaſing taxation, the extortions of the
" officials, and the heavy exactions of their own
" clergy." Not one man in a hundred of the
inhabitants knows how to read, and the chief
town Serajevo, which contains from 40,000 to
50,000 inhabitants, does not poſſeſs a ſingle
bookſeller's ſhop. And Von Thoemmel,
who was attached to the Auſtrian Conſulate
there for four years, ſays that " Nature has
" granted to theſe lands many fertile ſources of
" proſperity, but in mournful contraſt to the
" laviſhneſs of nature the people languiſh in deep
" dejection and poverty, frequently even in
" miſery."* Here we have French, Engliſh,
and German teſtimony borne to the miſerable
condition of the people under the curſe of miſ-
government, although ſoil, climate and poſition
are all favourable to happineſs and proſperity.

* Beſchreibung des Vilayet Boſnien, p. 211.

The population of Bofnia is chiefly agricultural. The peafants are maintained by and work
for the proprietors of the foil, and are very poor.*
The food of the people confifts chiefly of coarfe
bread, native cheefe, and vegetables, with very
rarely meat or poultry. The lodgings of the
artizans " an Englifh mechanic would confider
" uninhabitable. . . . . The houfes of the poorer
" claffes are mere hovels without any kind of
" comfort or accommodation, fituated in the
" midft of reeking filth, and as unhealthy as
" overcrowded and air-poifoned dwellings can
" poffibly be."† The climate, however, is
confidered good—cool and bracing in the mountainous parts, but "in the Herzegovina and
" other low fituations the heat is confiderable,
" and miafmatic fevers are frequent."‡

In the Confular Report on Bofnia for 1874 it
is ftated that " the general political condition of

* Confular Report for Bofnia, 1870.
† Ibid. ‡ Ibid.

" Bofnia during the paft year has been perfectly
" tranquil. .... What I have faid before
" regarding the adminiftration of the province
" ftill obtains. All amelioration is checked
" by the too frequent change of Governors.
" Dervifh Pafha [the prefent Governor] appears
" to be as good as moft of his predeceffors, but
" the uncertainty he feels as to his ftability in
" his poft naturally influences his conduct.
" Provincial affairs therefore are carried on as
" heretofore, and I fee no prefent profpect of
" improvement in profperity and civilifation."

As to roads, the fame Report fays, " road
" making has not been very actively carried on.
" The road from Serajevo to Moftar [in Herze-
" govina] begun ten years ago is ftill unfinifhed,
" though a certain progrefs has been made, and
" in dry weather it is now poffible to perform
" the journey in one of the rough carts of the
" country. .... The Brood road has not yet
" been repaired, though it is in a moft dilapi-

" dated condition, and in no other direction has
" any progreſs been made."

As to railways, " the propoſed railway through
" Boſnia is for the preſent in abeyance."

The revenue of the Province for 1874 was
eſtimated at £595,814, and the expenditure at
£197,514, ſhowing a balance of £398,300. In
theſe figures the cuſtom-houſe revenues are not
included, for they are always ſent to Conſtantinople and are never available for any provincial
neceſſities. Still with ſuch a ſurplus of income
over expenditure we are not ſurpriſed to learn
that " it never, or very rarely, happens that the
" income of the Province is inſufficient to cover
" all the outlay required of it." An income
and property tax has been eſtabliſhed in place of
the old perſonal tax called Verghi. There is
alſo a tax levied in ſubſtitution of military ſervice,
which has lately increaſed largely in total
amount.

The trade of Boſnia conſiſts chiefly of cereals,

wool and hides, but the cattle trade, once fo flourifhing in Bofnia, has entirely ceafed. Since the cattle difeafe firft broke out in 1862, it feems never to have thoroughly difappeared, and the Auftrian Government has ftrictly clofed the frontiers againft the importation of Bofnian cattle. " No notice of the difeafe feems to be taken " by the Turkifh authorities. It is admitted to " exift, but no efforts are made to check it, nor " are any reports made on the fubject."*

* Confular Report on Bofnia for 1874.

IV.

MONTENEGRO.

MONTENEGRO.

THE little State of Montenegro was in former times included in the Duchy of Zeta (fo called from the river Zeta or Zenta, which flows in it from north to fouth), and Zeta included part of Herzegovina. The native name of it is Tcherna Gora, " The Black Foreft," but the Venetians changed it to Montenegro, " The " Black Mountain," by which it is now known. Several derivations have been fuggefted for this epithet of " Black " applied to the State. One is that the Turks found the inhabitants fuch formidable opponents that they called it " The " Black Country." Another that it was an afylum for bandits and outlaws from the neigh-

H 2

bouring States, and thus became a receptacle of *Blackguards*; but this is a name wholly inapplicable to the Montenegrins, who are brave, courteous, and hofpitable; and at the little Court of Cetigné, the capital, the traveller will find culture and accomplifhments which would do honour to the moft civilifed nation of Europe. Another theory is that the epithet is owing to its gloomy rocks, which were formerly thickly covered with pines; another, that it is derived from the name of one of the oldeft rulers, Ivo Tfernöi (the Black). The Ottomans call the territory Karadagh, which means Black Mountain.

The country is a mafs of mountains of fantaftic forms, with vaft caverns in their fides and bafe, in which numbers of ftreams—they can hardly be called rivers—are loft to appear again after a fubterraneous paffage through the rocks. One writer has compared it to a petrified fea of mud, and another to an enormous cake of

PHYSICAL ASPECT.

wax perforated by a thoufand holes. According to an ancient legend, the Almighty at the creation of the world carried in a fack the rocks and mountains which he diftributed over the earth, but when over Montenegro the fack burft, and out fell the mountains in *pell-mell* confufion where they have remained ever fince. There are deep and narrow ravines which run up into the mountains, and in one part almoft cut the territory into two; thefe latter are held by the Turks, and at each end ftands a Turkifh fortrefs. The unwalled villages fcattered in the glens and on the flopes of the mountains are guarded by barriers of lofty rocks,—

——— "confufedly hurled,
Like fragments of an earlier world."

There is hardly anything which can be called a road in the territory. When the French occupied Dalmatia, the Emperor Napoleon offered to conftruct at his own expenfe a road from Kattaro to Nikfich, but the propofal was declined by the Montenegrins, who are naturally averfe to any fcheme which would make accefs to the interior of their country more eafy than it is. They know, too well, that they owe their freedom chiefly to the barrier of rocks and mountains which Nature has given them. It is in fact a country almoft impracticable to an enemy, as long as it is guarded by brave men.

But the climate is better than the rude afpect of the rocks denotes. On the level land to the fouth-eaft, on the borders of the Lake of Scutari, it has been compared to the climate of Nice, and figs, oranges, and olives grow there in abundance. In other parts there is good pafturage and plenty of corn.

Montenegro was part of ancient Illyricum, and fell under the dominion of Rome in the second century before Chrift. Traces of old Roman roads are ftill to be met with in the country. It continued to be part of the Roman Empire until it was attacked and conquered by the Goths, who, in turn, were fubdued by the Slavonic Serbs. It fhared the viciffitudes of the Dalmatian coaft, which was held in the middle ages at one time by Venice, and at another by Hungary, until the Servian power was fhattered at the battle of Kóffovo in 1389, as I have already mentioned. At that time it was governed by Prince Balfa, the fon-in-law of Lazar, the Kral or Defpot of Servia, to whofe affiftance he marched, but could not reach the camp in time to take part in the battle. Some Servian bands, under the leaderfhip of Strachina Ivo, furnamed Tfernoï (the Black), found a refuge after Kóffovo amongft the barren rocks of Montenegro. He married the fifter of Scanderbeg, the hero of Albania, and affifted him in his long conflict with the Ottoman Turks. In 1478, the Sultan Mahomet II. attacked Scutari, then held by the Venetians, and Ivo made a defcent upon Albania to effect a diverfion in favour of Venice. But the arms of the Sultan prevailed, and the Turks preffed forward to conquer Montenegro. Ivo went to Venice to demand fuccour, but the Republic had juft concluded peace with the Ottoman Porte, and his appeal was in vain. He returned to Montenegro, and abandoning his anceftral caftle of Jabliak, fituated on an ifland in the Lake of Scutari, took refuge in the mountains. He built a fort at Riéka and a church and convent at Cetigné, the prefent capital of Montenegro, and roufed fuch a fpirit of refiftance in the people that the Turks abandoned for the time the attempt at conqueft. His fon, George Tfernovich, however, who fucceeded him was lefs fortunate, and haraffed by the conftant irruptions of the Turks he determined in the year 1516 to abandon Monte-negro, and pafs the reft of his life in tranquillity at Venice, leaving the government in the hands of the *Vladika* or Metropolitan Bifhop of Cetigné.

From that time the Vladikas as Prince-Bifhops

became the rulers of Montenegro, and this ecclefiaftical form of government lafted for more than three hundred years. It became at laft hereditary in the family of Niégofch at the end of the feventeenth century. As every Vladika was confecrated Bifhop and could not marry, the fucceffion always paffed to a nephew, or fuch other member of the family as happened to be heir.

In 1623 Soleiman, Pacha of Scutari, pene-- trated to Cetigné, the capital, and " the fupre- " macy of the Sublime Porte was in name " eftablifhed over the Black Mountain. The " Ottomans, however, have never been able to " remain in poffeffion of the country." * By the Treaty of Carlowitz, 1699, Montenegro was left by the Ottomans under the protectorate of Venice. And by the Treaty of Paffarowitz, in 1718, it was in terms ceded back to Venice, and became again *nominally* fubject to the Porte.

---

* Twifs's Law of Nations, vol. i. § 73.

Its dependence on the Porte was recognifed by Auftria in the Treaty of Siftova in 1791; for that Treaty provides (Art. 1) that the in-habitants of Montenegro, Bofnia, Servia, Wal-lachia, and Moldavia, may re-enter their ancient poffeffions and enjoy their rights, without being punifhed or molefted " for having taken up " arms againft their own Sovereign, or for " having done homage to the Imperial Court " of Auftria."* This is important as bearing upon the claim of the Ottoman Porte, even now, to titular fovereignty over Montenegro, to which I fhall again allude.

In 1706 the Montenegrins placed themfelves formally under the protection of Rufia and took the oath of allegiance to the Czar, after which time it was ufual for each fucceffive Vladika to receive confecration at St. Peterfburg.

Under the fway of their Vladikas the in-habitants bravely and fuccefsfully refifted the

* Marten's Recueil, tom. v. 246.

repeated attempts of the Ottoman Porte to get poffeffion of the country. In the meantime not a few of them had apoftatized from the Chriftian faith and become followers of the Prophet, but under the rule of Daniel Petrovitch, the firft Vladika of the Niégofch family, and at his inftigation, the choice was given to these Muffulmans of either baptifm or death, and a fearful maffacre of moft of them took place.

The hiftory of the eighteenth century is a monotonous record of conftant hoftilities between the Montenegrins and the Turks, which have continued down to the prefent day. In 1716, the Montenegrins defeated two Turkifh Pachas, and drove their advancing troops out of the territory. But, in 1739, the Turks furrounded it on all fides, and for feven years completely blockaded every accefs to it. The mountaineers were fhut up amidft their inacceffible rocks, but they made frequent forties, and at laft fo haraffed their enemies that they retired, and left Montenegro for fome time unmolefted. In 1768, three Turkifh armies that invaded the country at different points were driven back, although the inhabitants had almost exhaufted all their ammunition, and were only able to obtain a fupply by making a foray during a terrible ftorm, and plundering one of the enemy's camps. During this century the Montenegrins were the victims of an impofture, by a perfon calling himfelf Peter III. of Ruffia, who was really dead, and he induced them to efpoufe his caufe, and obey him as their ruler, conjointly with their own Vladika. He however became blind, and retired to a monaftery, where he is faid to have been affaffinated.

In 1789 the Turks fuffered a fignal defeat. At that time Peter Petrovich Niégofch was the Vladika, and Mahmoud Pacha of Scutari, at the head of a numerous and powerful army, penetrated into the heart of Montenegro, but they were furrounded on all fides at Krouffa, and almoft entirely deftroyed by the mountaineers; the Pacha himfelf being amongft the flain. His head was long expofed to public view at Cetigné, and kept as a trophy of the victory. Peter Petrovich, who was as much diftinguifhed by his courage as his political wifdom, lived to a great age, and died in 1830. He had been able to wreft from the Pachalik of Scutari the rocky diftrict called Berda, which now forms part of Montenegro. He was fucceeded by his nephew of the fame name, a young man who at the time of the death of his uncle was only fifteen years of age. He was confecrated Vladika at St. Peterfburg in 1833, and he had hardly affumed the reins of power when he was called to defend his territory againft a furious onflaught of the Turks, led by the Pacha of Scutari. A great battle was fought in 1832, and the Montenegrins were victorious. This was followed by a peace of fome duration between Montenegro and Turkey, but foon afterwards fhe found herfelf engaged with another formidable enemy.

One of the greateft drawbacks to the profperity of the State is that it has no feaport. Antivari on the Adriatic, to the fouth of Montenegro, is the port of Scutari or Scudra, a Turkifh garrifon town, and can only be reached on the land fide through Turkifh territory. Cattaro, which feems defigned by nature to belong to Montenegro, and which lies to the north, at the head of a winding irregular gulf, called the *Bocche di Cattaro*, at a diftance from the frontier of only one hour's afcent up the mountain, belongs to Auftria. It is placed on a narrow ledge between the fea and the mountains, and its caftle is perched high above, amongft the rocks. A zig-zag road like a ladder climbs the mountain fide, and leads to the Montenegrin frontier, hardly more than a thousand yards in a direct line from the fea, and acrofs

the mountain it changes into a rough path as far
as Cetigné, the capital. Cattaro had been made
over by England to Montenegro, in return for
her co-operation with us in the war againſt
Napoleon, when the Montenegrins in 1814,
with the aid of a Britiſh fleet, attacked the
French at Cattaro and captured the town and
fortreſs. But they did not hold it long, for
after the termination of the war it was given
over at the Congreſs of Vienna to Auſtria, in
whoſe poſſeſſion it ſtill remains.

"The moſt important acquiſition for Monte-
"negro, and without which it will never make
"any real advance in civilization, is that of a
"ſeaport, however ſmall it may be, in order to
"have a direct and free communication with the
"reſt of the world, and indeed, it cannot but be
"a cauſe of conſtant heart-burning to the Monte-
"negrins to gaze on the ſea, which at Cattaro
"is ſeparated from their country by leſs than the
"diſtance of a rifle-ſhot, and not to have any

" accefs to it, except with the permiffion of the
"Auftrians."*

The poffeffion of Cattaro by Auftria led to a
collifion between that Power and Montenegro.
The mountaineers had, to ufe the term, "fquatted"
on the fea-coaft between Antivari and Cattaro,
and fo encroached upon Auftrian territory. The
Auftrian Government in 1838 fent its engineers
into Dalmatia to draw a frontier line, and as this
interfered with the fuppofed rights of the Montenegrins, they drove away the Auftrian officers,
and attacked fome Auftrian outpofts. To
avenge this infult a body of Auftrian troops
marched againft Montenegro, and an obftinate
engagement was fought in a mountain gorge in
which neither fide could claim a decifive fuccefs,
but the refult was that the Auftrians retired, and
in 1840 the queftion of the Montenegrin frontier
was referred to the arbitration of Ruffia, and

---

* Montenegro and the Slavonians of Turkey, by Count
Valerian Krafiufki. Quoted by Sir G. Wilkinfon.

peaceful relations were reftored between Monte-negro and Auftria.

The frontier of Montenegro had been for centuries ill-defined on the north, where the lowlands of Herzegovina join it, and was for a long time debatable ground. The inhabitants there are Rayas, that is, Chriftians under Turkifh rule; and their fympathies were, and ftill are, entirely with the Montenegrins. It has been always a difturbed diftrict, the fcene of conftant guerilla warfare between the two races, Chriftian and Turk, and in their ftruggles the Herzegovinian Rayas have looked to Monte-negro for help. Lord Strangford, who was our Ambaffador at Conftantinople, faid that Monte-negro has " a natural though limited line of " probable annexation on her north-weftern " frontier, in the Chriftian diftricts of the Herze-" govina towards Nikfich and Trebinje."*

* Quoted in Travels in the Slavonic Provinces, by Muir Mackenzie and Irby, p. 575.

The plain of Nikſich in Herzegovina is bounded
on the north by a range of mountains, which
were formerly covered with noble foreſts, now,
within the laſt few years, deſtroyed by the Turks.
" For eighteen months theſe mountains have
" been burning, and the magnificent oaks and
" beeches, which furniſhed the country around
" with the choiceſt timber, are now almoſt
" wholly deſtroyed. This has been done by
" orders from Conſtantinople, in order to form
" a ſterile frontier; but its effect will be to
" deſtroy the plain which lies at the foot of the
" mountains, and to reduce it to the condition
" of the arid plains of Albania on the other
" frontier of Montenegro." * There can be
little doubt that if the plain between Nikſich
and Montenegro were formally annexed, and
recogniſed as belonging, to Montenegro, it would
be better for her and Turkey alſo, for it would
put an end to a conſtant ſource of diſquiet and

* A Ride through Montenegro, by Rev. W. Denton, in 1865.

trouble, and by making the ruler of Montenegro directly refponfible for the peace of that diftrict as part of his dominions, it would remove the plaufible pretext which the Ottoman Porte too frequently has for charging him with fomenting difturbance on Turkifh territory.

The young Vladika died in 1851, and was fucceeded by Daniel I., who perifhed by the hand of an affaffin in 1860.

In 1852 Montenegro was attacked by the Turks under Omer Pacha, but the Auftrian Government interfered at Conftantinople, and by its mediation the expedition was recalled. During the Crimean war Prince Daniel obferved ftrict neutrality, notwithftanding the difturbed ftate of the Ottoman dominions in Europe, where the Chriftian population fympathifed with Ruffia, and in fome parts broke out in infurrection. He cherifhed the hope that at the Conference of Paris in 1856, his little kingdom would be formally recognifed as an independent

State For although Montenegro has never been fubftantially conquered by the Turks, and has never been for any length of time in their actual poffeffion, the Ottoman Porte ftill lays titular claim to it, and pretends that it is part of the Pachalik of Scutari. * In anfwer to Count Buol, at the Conference of Paris in 1856, Ali Pacha, the reprefentative of Turkey, faid that the Porte confidered Montenegro " as " an integral part of the Ottoman Empire, " although it had no intention of changing the " exifting ftate of things." This affertion was not negatived by any of the reprefentatives of the Great Powers, but provoked an indignant remonftrance from Prince Daniel, who, in a letter addreffed to the European Courts in May of that year, faid, " The affertion is un-

---

* We muft remember that our own fovereigns ftyled them-felves Kings of France until George III. dropped the abfurd title. And yet he had a better claim to it than the Turks ever had to the fuzerainty of Montenegro, for we once held for centuries a confiderable part of France.

" founded. The Montenegrins might with
" better right lay claim to half of Albania and
" the whole of Herzegovina ; becaufe my prede-
" ceffors, independent Princes of Montenegro,
" Dukes of Zeta, formerly poffeffed thofe terri-
" tories, whereas the Turks have never poffeffed
" Montenegro." I have faid that, by the Treaty
of Siftova, Montenegro was declared or admitted
by Auftria to be fubject to the Porte, and after
the fuccefsful foray of Soleiman Pacha in 1623,
the Turks laid claim to the fovereignty ; but
they were never able to hold poffeffion of the
country, and they feem to have had no more
real right by title of conqueft, than a nation at
war with another has a right to declare a paper
blockade, and fay that *jure gentium* it clofes the
enemy's ports.

In 1858, the Turks again attacked Montenegro with a powerful armament, and the diftrict
of Grahovo, bordering on Herzegovina, was the
fcene of a decifive battle, in which the Monte-

negrins were victorious. In a despatch by
Mirko Petrovich, the brother of Prince Daniel,
and the general who commanded in the action,
he said, " Of the thousands of which the Turkish
" army was composed, scarce a few hundreds
" have escaped to tell how the Montenegrins
" can fight for their country. Your soldiers
" have slain seven thousand Turks, taken eight
" pieces of artillery, twelve hundred caparisoned
" horses, and five hundred tents. . . . It is thus
" that the Montenegrins have in part avenged
" the defeat of their Servian ancestors on the
" plain of Kóssovo on June 15, 1389."

A delimitation of frontiers was made between
Montenegro and Turkey in 1842 ; and in 1858
the question came under discussion at a conference of Ambassadors in Constantinople, where
they met to consider the report of a Commission
that had been appointed to determine the actual
limits of the territory. This Commission was
composed of delegates from England, France,

Auftria, Pruffia, Ruffia, Turkey, and Montenegro, and had met at Scutari in the fummer of
1857. Ali Pacha wifhed to infert in the Protocol an affertion of the right of fovereignty of
the Ottoman Porte over Montenegro; but this
was ftrongly oppofed by the reprefentatives of
France and Ruffia, and the refult was that the
Protocol was figned without any infertion of the
obnoxious claim. The fouthern limit of Montenegro was fixed by a line beginning at a point
due north of, but clofe to Antivari: it paffes
through the weftern part of the Lake of Scutari,
and extends to the eaft as far as the Graditchnita
river. The northern frontier extends from a
point fouth-weft of Grahovo, near Dalmatia, as
far as Brucovi in the eaft.* A glance at the
official map fhows that the territory is pinched,
like the body of a wafp, in the middle; Herzegovina preffing into it on the north and Albania

* See Hertflet's Map of Europe by Treaty, 1814–1875, vol. ii.
p. 1354.

on the fouth. This delimitation of frontiers was confirmed by a Protocol between Turkey and Montenegro on the 26th of October, 1866. It was provided in the *procès verbal* of 1858 that " the demarcation fhall in no way interfere with " the private property poffeffed on either fide of " the frontiers, either by individuals or by vil- " lages."*

In 1861, hoftilities again broke out between the Turks and Montenegrins, in which, as ufual, the inhabitants of the fouthern part of Herzegovina were involved. Prince Daniel was now dead, and had been fucceeded by his nephew, Prince Nicholas, the fon of Mirko Petrovitch. Omer Pacha was fent from Conftantinople with inftructions to reftore order in the difturbed diftricts by negotiation or force of arms. With him was affociated a commiffion reprefenting the five Great Powers, the members of which had an

---

* See Hertflet's Map of Europe by Treaty, 1814–1875, vol. iii. p. 1787.

interview with the Montenegrin and Herzegovinian chiefs ; but it led to no definite refult.
Prince Nicholas offered to affift in the pacifica-
tion of Herzegovina on three conditions : 1. The
recognition by Turkey of the independence of
Montenegro ; 2. The grant of a feaport ;
3. The rectification of frontiers. But thefe
propofals were not favourably received, and the
commiffion was fhortly afterwards diffolved.
The quarrel now became open war. The
Montenegrins attacked the Turkifh town of
Kernitza, in Albania, and compelled the troops
there to furrender, carrying them prifoners to
Cetigné, where they were kindly treated, and
moft of them were foon afterwards fet at liberty.
Omer Pacha vigoroufly preffed on the war.
Mirko Petrovitch, the father of Prince Nicholas,
and elder brother of the former Prince Daniel,
took the military command of the Montenegrins, and obftinate battles were fought in which
the mountaineers, men, women, and children,

defended their country with heroic courage. But the Turks gained fome fenfible advantages, and at one time a report was fpread through Europe that Cetigné, the capital of Montenegro, had been taken. But it was taken only in a lying Turkifh map.

At laft peace was reftored, and in 1862 a Convention was figned at Scutari, which has for the time fettled the quarrel between Montenegro and the Porte. In the Convention not a word is faid about the pretenfions of Turkey to fovereignty over Montenegro. The limits affigned to the territory by the Protocol of 1858 were confirmed; but there was an important provifion which bears upon the prefent ftruggle going on in Herzegovina. By the feventh article it was agreed that the Montenegrins fhould make no hoftile expeditions outfide their frontiers, and "in cafe of infurrection in any of "the adjoining diftricts they were to give it no "fupport, either moral or material." Montenegro alfo engaged not to erect any tower or fortification on the confines of Albania, Bofnia, or Herzegovina. And there was to be a mutual extradition of criminal fugitives from juftice.

The prefent Conftitution of Montenegro is that contained in the Code of Prince Daniel, promulgated in 1855. This Code embraces not only the Conftitution, but alfo the civil and criminal law of the State. The Government had, as I have before mentioned, been half ecclefiaftical and half civil; but now the hereditary fovereignty was vefted in the family of Niégofch in the male line as fecular Princes. The title of the Prince in the Montenegrin language is "Kniaze and Gofpodar (*i e.* Hofpodar) of "Tchernagora and Berda." * The Code eftablifhed alfo a Senate, *Soviet,* confifting of eighteen members, from amongft whom the Prince choofes his Council of Minifters. The

* Berda, or properly B'rda, means a group of rocky mountains.

Senate prepares laws for his fanction, and acts as a Supreme Court of Juftice. But the old Slavonic principle of regard for popular rights remains, and every village or department has the right of electing its own chiefs. It will be interesting to quote from Krafinfki a paffage which defcribes the mode in which public bufinefs was carried on at the time he wrote : * " In a femi-
" circular recefs formed by the rocks on one
" fide of the plain of Tfetinie, and about half
" a mile to the fouthward of the town, is a
" level piece of grafs land with a thicket of low
" poplar-trees. Here the Diet is held; from
" which the fpot has received the name of *Mali*
" *S'bor*, ' the fmall affembly.' When any matter
" is to be difcuffed the people meet in this their
" *Runnimede*, or ' meadow of Council,' and
" partly on the level fpace, partly on the rocks,
" receive from the Vladika notice of the queftion

* Cited by Sir G. Wilkinfon in his Travels in Dalmatia and Montenegro.

" propofed. The duration of the difcuffion is
" limited to a certain time, at the expiration of
" which the affembly is expected to come to
" a decifion; and when the bell of the monaftery
" orders filence, notwithftanding the moft ani-
" mated difcuffion, it is inftantly reftored. The
' Metropolitan afks again what is their decifion,
" and whether they agree to his propofal? The
" anfwer is (generally) the fame, *Budi po tvoyemu,*
" *Vladika,* ' Let it be as thou wifheft, O
" ' Vladika ! ' "

The population of Montenegro is about
120,000, and it contains from eighty to ninety
geographical fquare miles. It is divided into
eight *Nátuas,* or diftricts, and thefe again into
plémenes, or communes.

There is no regular army, but all the male
inhabitants who can carry arms are ready at a
moment's notice to fight in defence of their
country. The number of thefe, between the
ages of twenty and fifty years, is eftimated at

20,000; and in a territory fo impregnable by nature, they are amply fufficient to repel an attacking force, unlefs in overwhelming numbers.

The Montenegrins ufed to have a favage cuftom of difplaying the fkulls of their enemies flain in battle, and above the monaftery of Tfetinie ftood a famous Tower of Skulls, where thefe ghaftly trophies were hung up. But the tower has been pulled down, and the monaftery is now better known by its printing-prefs.

One characteriftic of the people is the refpect fhown to women. Not that they do not labour hard and carry enormous loads, but they need fear neither infult nor injury. It is faid that a young girl may travel from one end of Monte-negro to the other in perfect fafety, and her prefence protects even an enemy from outrage.*

It is impoffible not to feel fympathy and refpect for this diminutive Highland State, which, furrounded on three fides—the north, eaft, and

* Les Serbes en Turquie, Ubicini, p. 151.

fouth—by the Turkifh provinces of Herzegovina, Bofnia, and Albania, has gallantly held its
own for centuries againft all the efforts of the
Ottoman Porte. Over and over again it has
been attacked, but it has never been really conquered. The tide of Turkifh invafion has
furged in vain againft the rocks of the Black
Mountain, and the Montenegrins ftand a free
and Chriftian people in the midft of countries
which have long fuccumbed to the rule of an
Infidel Power. The name of Marathon ftands
out glorious in all time, for there a handful of
Greeks crufhed an invading hoft—Perfia "and
"all her chivalry;"—and Grahovo deferves an
almoft equal place in the Temple of Fame, for
there a handful of mountaineers rolled back the
torrent of Turkifh invafion, and maintained their
anceftral freedom againft the laft defperate effort
of the Ottoman Porte. Who will not hope that
their independence may remain fecure, and that the
Crefcent there will never triumph over the Crofs?

V.

BULGARIA.

BULGARIA.

BULGARIA, which adjoins Servia on the eaſt, is that part of Turkey which in the days of the Roman Empire was known as Mœſia. It is ſeparated from Roumelia on the ſouth by the lofty range of the Balkan Mountains. The north-eaſtern portion of it is called the Dobroufcha, and a railway croſſes it from Ruſtchuk on the Danube to Varna on the Black Sea. It is the moſt deſolate line by which I ever travelled, paſſing through a country the features of which reminded me of the Suſſex Downs, but with no ſmiling villages, and hardly any viſible population.   ·

The whole province is now compriſed in the

Vilayet of Touna on the Danube, but this feems to be compofed of three divifions—thofe of Siliftria, Widdin and Niffa.

Gibbon does not make it clear whether he confiders the Bulgarians and Slavonians as the fame or different races. He fays, " The wild " people who dwelt or wandered in the plains of " Ruffia, Lithuania, and Poland, might be reduced " in the age of Juftinian under the two great " families of Bulgarians and the Slavonians."*
He fpeaks of their " *Tartar* manners," but fays that the Bulgarians affumed a vague dominion over the Slavonian name, and then in a general defcription of the Slavonians confounds them and the Bulgarians together. And yet afterwards he fpeaks of them as different, and fays that he does not attempt to define their intermediate boundaries, which were not accurately known or refpected by the barbarians themfelves. Again he fays, " I adopt the appellation of Bulgarians.

* Decline and Fall, chap. 42.

". . . The name of Huns is too vague; the
"tribes of the Cutturgarians and Utturgarians
"are too minute and too harſh." He ſpeaks of
"an invaſion of the Huns or Bulgarians, ſo
"dreadful that it almoſt effaced the memory of
"their paſt inroads." But immediately afterwards he treats them as Slavonians, who having
"inſolently divided themſelves into two bands,
"diſcovered the weakneſs and miſery of a
"triumphant reign." Again, "In the thirty-
"ſecond winter of Juſtinian's reign, the Danube
"was deeply frozen; Zahergan led the cavalry
"of the Bulgarians, and his ſtandard was fol-
"lowed by a promiſcuous multitude of Slavo-
"nians."* They advanced againſt Conſtantinople, but were met and defeated by the aged
Beliſarius, and after ravaging the plains of
Thrace retired upon the Danube.

The truth is that the Bulgarians were not
properly a Slavonic tribe, although Gibbon ſays,

* Decline and Fall, chap. 43.

133

" The unqueftionable evidence of language
" attefts the defcent of the Bulgarians from the
" original ftock of the Sclavonian, or more pro-
" perly Slavonian race ; and the kindred bands
" of Servians, Bofnians, Rafcians, Croatians,
" Wallachians, &c. followed either the ftandard or
" the example of the leading tribe." *

Schafarik, however, relies upon the " unquef-
" tionable evidence of language " to prove that
the Bulgarians were originally different from
the Slavs.†

He defcribes the Bulgarians, the Avars, the
Huns and other tribes as *Baftardvölker* formed
by an intermingling of the Mongolian and

* Decline and Fall, chap. 55.

† Slavifche Alterthümer, ii. 29. He fays that many writers
have defcribed the Bulgarians as originally Slavs, but incorrectly.
He combats the opinion with much learning, but it is unneceffary here to go through his reafons. I may mention, however, that he relies ftrongly on the old names of Bulgarian chiefs
and towns, as fhowing the difference of the language from
Slavonic, and fays that there are ftill to be found amongft the
Slavonic races in Turkey words of Bulgarian origin, the roots of
which are unknown to the Slavs.

Finnish stocks with old Turkish blood.* He
considers them as distinct from the Slavs, and
says that they and other Uralian-Turkish tribes
from the lower Volga and the Don pressed upon
the Slavs and drove them to the west and south.†
But he afterwards calls them Bulgarian Slavs
when they had overrun Mœsia, and says that
the Slavs there lost their proper name and received that of their conquerors, Bl'gare. The
fact was that the two tribes coalesced like the
Normans and Saxons in England, and formed
ultimately one people. The change was, as
might be expected, gradual, and the intermix-
ture of the races was not complete until the
ninth century, from which period we may treat
the Bulgarians as part of the Slavonic nation.

But the name of the dominant race whose
language has prevailed never superseded that

---

* Slavische Alterthümer, i. 5. In one of the oldest Sagas the
name Bolgar appears as Borgar, Ib. i. 8.

† Ibid. ii. 6.

of the people with whom they blended. That part of Turkey in Europe where the Bulgarians firſt ſettled has always been, and ſtill is, called Bulgaria, although the pure Bulgarian element of the population has long ceaſed to exiſt. It may be likened to the caſe of Britain, which retains the name it bore before the Anglo-Saxons invaded the ſoil and the old Celtic race of Britons in England dwindled away, until at laſt they were found only in the mountains of Wales and receſſes of Cornwall.

From the ſeventh to the tenth century the Bulgarians were firmly eſtabliſhed as a powerful nation ſouth of the Danube in what was the old Roman Province of Mœſia Inferior, once occupied by the Getæ, the earlieſt inhabitants of whom we have any record. According to Suidas their leader Terbeles impoſed tribute upon two Greek Emperors, but in 811 Nicephorus invaded their territory. His camp was ſurpriſed by the Bulgarians, and the Emperor was ſlain. His skull, enchased with gold, was often used at their feasts; "but they were softened before the end "of the same century by a peaceful intercourse "with the Greeks, the possession of a cultivated "region, and the introduction of the Christian "worship."* One of their most distinguished rulers in the early part of the ninth century was Simeon, a youth of the royal line, who had originally been a monk before he ascended the throne. He governed Bulgaria for more than forty years, and was repeatedly engaged in war with the Greek Empire. At one time he besieged Constantinople, and dictated terms of peace to the Emperor. The rulers of Bulgaria were then gratified by the high founding title accorded to them of Basileus, King or Emperor, and for some time peace prevailed. But at the end of the tenth century war again broke out, when the Bulgarians were conquered by Basil II., and so merciless and terrible was the slaughter

* Gibbon, Decline and Fall, chap. 55.

that the Emperor acquired the title of "Slayer of the Bulgarians" (Βουλγαροκτόνος). "The " Bulgarians were fwept away from their fettle- " ments, and circumfcribed within a narrow " province ; the furviving chiefs bequeathed to " their children the advice of patience and the " duty of revenge." *

For more than a century and a half they remained in a ftate of fervitude to the Greek Empire until the reign of Ifaac Angelus, when, provoked by injury and oppreffion, they rofe in revolt in 1186, and under their leader Calo-John or Joannice recovered their independence. John fent an embaffy to the Pope Innocent III., profeffing himfelf to be a fon of the Latin Church, and he received from the Vatican the grant of a royal title, while at the fame time a Latin Archbifhop was fent into Bulgaria.

The Bulgarians feem to have ofcillated for many years between the rival claims of the

* Gibbon, Decline and Fall, chap. 55.

Greek and Latin Churches. They fent an Embaffy to Rome in 866 and afked for Bifhops and priefts, and books and facred veftments, and their requeft was complied with. But at the fame time the Greek Patriarch tried hard to induce them to join the Greek Communion—and at the Council of Conftantinople (869-870) four Bulgarian deputies appeared, and Bulgaria was declared to be under the Patriarchate.

I have mentioned that it recovered its independence at the latter end of the twelfth century, and this it maintained until the middle of the fourteenth, when it became fubjeƈt to Hungary. But in 1392 the Turks wrefted it from the Hungarians, and fince then it has remained a Turkifh province.

As fuch it has hardly a hiftory, and it would be to little purpofe to relate abortive attempts at infurreƈtion. I will come to times of recent date. When the French Revolutionary War broke out, and the Ottoman Porte was engaged in hoftilities with Ruffia and Auftria, Bulgaria became the fcene of much difturbance. Bands of Bulgarian volunteers enrolled themfelves under the leaderfhip of Omer Pafvan, and attacked the Auftrian pofts in Servia, but having quarrelled with the Pacha of Widdin and being accufed of blafphemy againft the Koran, he was put to death by the executioner. His fon of the fame name efcaped, and put himfelf at the head of free-lances, who were joined by deferters from the Janiffaries, and he made himfelf mafter of Widdin. The Bulgarian Rayas were allowed to take up arms againft Omer Pafvan, and for ten years a fort of civil war raged in the province. In vain a Turkifh army befieged Widdin, and when it retired Bulgaria became the prey of robber bands commanded by Omer Pafvan, who ravaged the country in every direction, and entering Servia committed atrocious outrages againft the Rayas there. They took Belgrade, and I have already told how the Janiffary Dahis were routed and put to death in Servia. The remnant of Pafvan's followers, a fcanty band, found their way back to Widdin in 1805. Pafvan however was fo far fuccefsful, that he was recognifed by the Porte as Vizier of Bulgaria, and after his death he was fucceeded in the fame office by his former fecretary, who was known as Molla Pacha.

By the Treaty of Buchareft (May, 1812) Beffarabia was given to Ruffia, but Servia and Bulgaria were to remain under the fovereignty of the Ottoman Porte. Molla Pacha was deprived of his Vizierfhip, and the government of Bulgaria was beftowed upon Huffein Pacha, who proved himfelf to be an oppreffive and rapacious ruler of the unfortunate Rayas.

When the Ruffians entered Bulgaria in 1828 they were hailed as deliverers, and their victories over the Turks were celebrated by folemn chaunts in the Chriftian churches of the country. But the inhabitants would not take up arms, and join the Ruffians in active warfare. After peace was concluded by the Treaty of Adrianople in 1829, the Ruffians carried with them acrofs the Danube great numbers of the Bulgarian Rayas who had been moft deeply compromifed in the ftruggle, and affigned them lands along the banks of the Dnieper. But the love of their native country was too ftrong, and gradually they all returned to Bulgaria.

A fecret fociety was now formed in the neighbourhood of Ternov. The members met in the receffes of the forefts, pretending to be engaged in religious fêtes, and in the graveyards of the convents fwore on the tombs of their anceftors that they would die for their country. They were, however, betrayed, and many of their leaders arrefted and put to death. In 1838 an infurrection broke out, and Jarnoï, which was garrifoned by the Turks, was attacked. The infurgents relied on help from Servia, but Milofch amufed them with promifes which led to nothing. A few unimportant reforms in the focial and municipal fyftem, conceded by the Sultan, were the only fruits of the movement, and even thefe were foon practically fet afide.

M. Cyprien Robert, in an interefting article on Bulgaria in the *Revue des Deux Mondes* (1842) begins by faying, " On the confines of " Europe there vegetates, enflaved and unfor- " tunate, a nation hardly known by name at " the prefent day, and yet deferving all our " intereft. This nation is that of the Bulgarians; " it has preferved in the hardeft ftate of flavery " its ancient manners, its lively faith, its noble " character, and after having had a glorious paft, " it feems ftill called upon, by its geographical " pofition, to play an important part in the " future."

Bulgaria has been little explored by travellers, and a general opinion has prevailed that the inhabitants are coarfe and churlifh, as if they were part of the fame people of whom Goldfmith fays,—

> " the rude Carinthian boor
> Againft the houfelefs ftranger fhuts the door."

But nothing can be more untrue.

An Englifh traveller, Dr. Walfh, fays, " Of " all the peafantry I have ever met with, the " Bulgarians feem the moft fimple, kind and " affectionate, forming a ftriking contraft with " the rude and brutal Turks, who are mixed " amongft them, but diftinguifhed by the " ftrongeft traits of character. . . . The " Bulgarians were diftinguifhed by caps of brown " fheepfkin ; jackets of cloth made of the wool " undyed of dark brown fheep, which their " wives fpin and weave; white cloth troufers, " and fandals of brown leather, drawn under the " fole and laced with thongs under the inftep ; " and they carried neither piftol nor yatigan, nor " any other weapon of offence ; but they were " ftill more diftinguifhed by their countenance

144

" and demeanour. The firſt is open, artleſs and
" benevolent ; and the ſecond is ſo kind and
" cordial that every one we met ſeemed to wel-
" come us as friends. . . . Turkiſh women
" we never ſaw ; the Bulgarian women mixed
" freely with us in the domeſtic way, and treated
" us with the unſuſpecting cordiality they would
" ſhow to brothers. . . . Their villages
" generally conſiſt of forty or fifty houſes,
" ſcattered without order or regularity. Their
" houſes are built of wicker-work plaſtered, and
" are clean and comfortable in the inſide." And
M. Cyprien Robert, who travelled much in the
country, ſays that all who know Bulgaria praiſe
with one voice the peaceful virtues of the inhabitants. " They are induſtrious, perſevering,
" and temperate, and although the moſt oppreſſed
" of all the ſubject races, miſery has not debaſed
" them." Their honeſty is ſuch that a Bulgarian may be truſted with large ſums of money
with perfect ſecurity. In intelligence they are

145   L

rather flow, and want the quicknefs and vivacity of their Servian neighbours.

Bulgaria is one of the moft fertile countries in Europe, and agriculture is the chief occupation. It is in fact one of the chief granaries of the Ottoman Empire. But the inhabitants manufacture rifle-barrels and coarfe ftuffs, and cultivate immenfe quantities of rofes, from which they diftil the famous *attar* of rofes.

Each Bulgarian Commune has its Turkifh Governor or *Spahi*, who is often an abfentee, and makes ufe of a middleman to collect his dues and enforce his rights, fuch for inftance as the *corvée* or three days' forced labour from each peafant every year.

Bulgaria had two capitals; Ternov, where its kings refided, and Sofia (originally Sardika), which feems to bear the fame relation to Ternov that Mofcow does to St. Peterfburgh. It is the facred city of the Bulgarians, round which their traditions moft fondly cling. It is fituated in the fouth-weft, furrounded by almoft inacceffible mountains, and, as the name implies, was once a city of the Greek Empire. But it has fallen into decay—its ftreets are almoft deferted, and what was once a Chriftian Cathedral is now a Turkifh Mofque.

Writing in 1842 M. Cyprien Robert fays that when he travelled in Bulgaria, the Chriftian population concealed as much as poffible their religious worfhip from the Turks, to efcape outrage at their hands. In fome places the churches were mere *crypts*, or miferable hovels —and no convent or church when falling into decay could be repaired without permiffion from the Divan, which could not be obtained without payment of an exorbitant fum. All the privileges from time to time accorded by the Porte had been loft, and the condition of the people depended upon the caprice of the Pachas. But the cafe was different with the population amongft the mountain ranges, for there the *haïdouks*, or brigands as they are called, were able to fecure for themfelves a fort of independence.* We muft not, however, confound thefe with ordinary brigands. They take arms to defend themfelves againft the rapacity and outrages of the Turks—and of courfe are vilified by them under an opprobrious name.

* Le Monde Gréco-Slave. Revue des Deux Mondes, 1842.

VI.

TURKISH GOVERNMENT.

VI.

TURKISH GOVERNMENT.

THE whole of Turkey in Europe is divided into fifteen *Eyalets*, or *Vilayets*, as they are called in Weftern Europe, that is, Adminif- trative Divifions; and thefe are fubdivided into provinces, called *livas* or *fandjaks*. There is a further fubdivifion of the *fandjaks* into *cazas* or diftricts, and the *cazas* are again divided into *nahiyés*, compofed of villages and hamlets.

The Principality of Servia, although practi- cally independent, is ftill included by the Otto- man Porte in the vilayet of Roumelia; and the Khedive of Egypt alfo finds himfelf nominally in a vilayet. The vilayet of Bofnia comprifes alſo Herzegovina and Turkiſh Croatia. Bulgaria is in the vilayet of the Danube called Touna.

The Rayas or Raïahs (plural of *ra'yet*, a flock) are the non-Muſſulman population of Turkey, including, therefore, all the Chriſtians.

The male population of Turkey in Europe, according to the cenſus of 1873, is 8,396,005, thus divided :—

Chriſtians .	. 4,701,357
Muſſulmans .	3,619,353
Jews	. . 75,295
	8,396,005

The uſual form of municipal government is the following. There is a Turkiſh Governor of the diſtrict, who is called *mudir* or *kaimakan*, and he is generally an Oſmanli Muſſulman, who buys his office from the Sultan. He is aſſiſted by a council of *medjlis*, who, with the exception of a ſingle Chriſtian Raya, or in ſome caſes two, are all Muſſulmans, and the *mudir's* court has excluſive criminal juriſdiction. The head or reprefentative of each Chriftian community is its chief elder, called in the Turkifh language *kodgia bafhi*, who acts as judge in civil cafes, and is elected by the Chriftians themfelves. The Rayas in general avoid the towns, where they are moft expofed to Turkifh infolence and aggreffion, and refide in the country and villages.

There are four principal taxes in Turkey, which I will now defcribe.

The firft is the *afhr*, a tax of one-tenth on all agricultural produce. It is the principal item of revenue, and produced in 1869 £5,641,245. The right of collecting this tax is fold to the higheft bidder. The farmers of it buy each a whole *fandjak,* and fell their bargains in lots to others, who again fub-divide their lots to others, and on each of thefe fales a profit muft of courfe be made. This fyftem is called *iltizam.*

" The profits made in this way by the higher
" contractors are known to be enormous, and
" have been the foundation of the largeft for-

" tunes in Turkey. This traffic is generally
" purfued by ' rayas,' or even foreign fubjects,
" but always requires for fuccefs the affiftance
" and connivance, often the fecret participation,
" of an influential Turk at head-quarters." *
The fyftem has been denounced by all, or nearly
all, competent authorities. " Whole diftricts
" have thus been, and are now being, firft im-
" poverifhed and ultimately depopulated." And
to fhow how wafteful is the fyftem to the public
treafury, I may mention that in the *fandjak* of
Rouftchouk, in Bulgaria, the tithes were fold in
1869 for £270,000 ; but only realized to the
Government £180,000, owing to the contractors
being unable to pay the ftipulated prices. It
reminds one of the ruinous competition for land
that ufed to prevail in Ireland, when farmers
offered rents for leafes which they were utterly

---

* Report on the Taxation of Turkey, by Mr. Barron, H.M.
Secretary to the Embaffy, prefented to both Houfes of Parliament, May, 1870.

unable to pay and make anything like a profit.
" As a tax the tithe itſelf is radically vicious in
" principle, and oppoſed to all ſound economical
" doctrines, being levied on the groſs, not on the
" net, produce of the ſoil, and taking no account
" of the relative coſt of production."

A modification has, however, been recently
introduced in favour of the peaſants. This
conſiſts in ſelling the tithes in every village ſepa-
rately, and thus permitting the " Commune " to
declare itſelf the purchaſer at the maximum price
attained by the biddings. And every State
functionary is prohibited, under penalties, from
bidding for the tithes directly or indirectly.

Another tax is the *verghi*, raiſed on property
and income; which is fixed beforehand at a
certain amount for each province, and is then
apportioned among the ſandjaks and other ſubordinate diviſions by the provincial authorities.
The apportionment, however, is not annual, and
" the ſub-allotment of the tax among individuals

" is not governed by any law or fixed prin-
"ciple."* In the village *medjlis*, or councils,
it offers the wideſt ſcope for favoritiſm, for
tyranny towards the weak, and truckling to the
ſtrong. " Everywhere the apportionment is
" arbitrary. In ſhort, it may be ſaid that this
" tax in no way affects the richer claſſes, the
" middle but ſlightly, and falls, ſo to ſpeak,
" altogether on the pooreſt."

A third tax is the *haratch*, which falls exclu-
ſively upon the non-Muſſulman ſubjects of the
Porte, in conſideration of their exemption from
military ſervice. It is eſtimated to produce an
annual ſum of more than half a million. " It is
" not eaſy to learn what data the Government
" poſſeſſes for apportioning this impoſt among
" the *vilayets* and provinces."

The remaining tax is the *ſaymé*, a tax origi-

* Report on the Taxation of Turkey, by Mr. Barron, H.M.
Secretary to the Embaſſy, preſented to both Houſes of Parliament, May, 1870.

nally on sheep and goats, but afterwards extended to swine and cattle. It is a sort of equivalent impost on pasture lands for the tithe which is payable on arable land, and amounts to ten per cent. on the average value of the sheep.

One characteristic of land tenure in Turkey is the immense quantity of land which is held in *Vakouf*, that is, in a kind of mortmain, consecrated to religion, and belonging to mosques or holy places. In order to escape from the oppression of the tax-gatherer it is not uncommon for the Raya proprietor to make over his land in Vakouf to a mosque, under an implied trust, and to cultivate it himself as a farmer or labourer employed by the priests of the mosque.

It would be a mistake to suppose that the Christians are the only part of the population that is oppressed and miserable. Turkish misgovernment is uniform, and falls with a heavy hand upon all alike. In some parts of the kingdom the poverty of the Mussulmans may be actually worfe than the poverty of the Chriftians, and it is *their* condition which moft excites the pity of the traveller. It is indeed an inftructive fact that whenever a writer on Turkey fixes his attention on any particular part of the population, he defcribes it as the moft miferable of all. M. Cyprien Robert fays that the Chriftians in the Eaft have, with a few noble exceptions, no greater enemies than their monks (*moines*), who profit by the oppreffion of the people, and fhare with the Turk the impofts laid upon the Rayas. " The firft meafure of regeneration would be the " reform of the clergy." *

But it is untrue to affert that the fufferings of the Muffulmans are anywhere equal to the fufferings of the Chriftians. Common fenfe tells us that where there is a fanatical dominant population infpired with hatred and contempt of a fubfervient race, the fcales of juftice and equity can never be held evenly between them. And to all the

* Le Monde Greco-Slave, Revue des Deux Mondes, 1862.

miſery which the Muſſulman has to endure from his own poverty and the rapacity of officials, is to be added in the caſe of the Chriſtian the inſolence and brutality of a governing claſs. Whatever may be the theory of equality laid down in Firmans, and Hats, and Iradés, and Hatti-Sheriffs, the Turk never has treated, and never will treat, the Giaour as an equal. I will mention an anecdote related by Miſs Irby, by way of illuſtration of this. A Derviſh met in the road near Serajevo (Boſna Serai), the capital of Boſnia, a Pravoſlav prieſt on horſeback. He ordered him to diſmount, ſaying, " Boſnia is ſtill a " Mahommedan country ; do you not ſee that a " Turk is paſſing? Diſmount inſtantly!" Three different times the Derviſh met the ſame prieſt, and each time obliged him to get off his horſe. If we wiſh to know how the pompous profeſſions of the Sultan have been realiſed, we muſt gather information from the diſtant provinces of the Empire, and ſee what is the actual condition of

the Rayas there. And very recently we have
been furnifhed with authentic facts from Bulgaria,
which fhow how groffly they are outraged.
Chriftian women are violated, and Chriftian
men are tortured by Turkifh mifcreants with
impunity. I will cite two inftances out of many
which have recently appeared in Turkifh news-
papers—as told in a letter written from Efki-
Zaghra.

At Sulmuchli "the Turks have broken into
" the houfes of the Bulgarians, where they
" violated half a fcore of young girls and three
" young married women. They killed twelve
" Bulgarians and wounded eight; then, as they
" withdrew, they took away with them the corn,
" the lighter furniture, and all the portable pro-
" perty of the Chriftian inhabitants.

" In the village of Cafanka, three hours and a
" half diftant from Efki-Zaghra, the rural guard,
" with two zaptiehs, or policemen, and other
" Turks, arrefted fifteen Bulgarians, fhut them

"up in a hut, and putting knives to their "throats, extorted 46 Turkiſh lire (the lira is "equal to 18*s*. 2*d*.)." *

It would be eaſy to multiply caſes of Turkiſh outrage not only in Bulgaria but in Boſnia ; and in the latter province there is the peculiarity I have before alluded to, that the Muſſulman population there, with the exception of a few officials, are not Oſmanli Turks, but deſcendants of Chriſtians who in former times apoſtatized from their faith, and who are diſtinguiſhed by their rancour againſt the Rayas. Hence, ſays Profeſſor A. Vambéry, in an article in a leading German Review :—"The genuine Turk is not ſo much "hated by the Chriſtians as the Slavonic Muſ-"ſulman." Nor ought we to forget that the poor Rayas ſuffer much from their co-religioniſts. If we may truſt the teſtimony of eye-witneſſes, they are fleeced by their Biſhops and prieſts ;

* Quoted by the Special Correſpondent of the *Times* in a letter dated Pera, Dec. 31, 1875.

and the Chriftians who fit amongft the Medjlis, or municipal councils, are generally worthlefs creatures, who cringe to their Turkifh mafters, and betray the caufe of their Chriftian brethren. Altogether the picture of the ftate of the Rayas in the Slavonic provinces of Turkey is moft deplorable, and I do not believe it ever can be effectually ameliorated until Turkifh domination is put an end to.

Hitherto none but Muffulmans have been liable to confcription for military fervice. And this, of courfe, was not out of favour to the Chriftian Rayas, but from fear of admitting them into the ranks and accuftoming them to the ufe of arms. They confiderably outnumber the Muffulman population, and the Government knows too well that they have good caufe for difaffection. We can hardly, therefore, blame a policy which has been dictated by an inftinct of felf-defence, and which is neceffary fo long as the oppreffion of a Government makes it unfafe to truft the greater part of its fubjects with arms.

As to the admiffion of Chriftian fubjects of the Porte into the army, although it is true that the Hatti Humayoum of 1856 expreffly declared that in future there fhould be no difference between Rayas and Muffulmans, and all alike fhould be liable to ferve, it is equally true that "thefe clear provifions of the organic law have "been hitherto entirely ignored." * Fuad Pacha explained this in 1866 by the alleged repugnance of the non-Muffulmans to enter the military fervice; but he declared that it was the intention of the Government to carry out the meafure, and, he faid, "there exift, moreover, already in "the Ottoman army two regiments of mixed "Coffacks, compofed of Muffulmans and Chrif- "tians." It is not, however, furprifing that the Chriftians themfelves are little covetous of

* Report on the Taxation of Turkey by Mr. Barron, H.M. Secretary to the Embaffy.

the honour of being liable to confcription, and we are told, on authority, that the *Haratch* is probably the only tax which is paid with cheerful alacrity. And Mr. Barron, in his Report on the Taxation of Turkey, dwells on the " mifery en-" tailed on the Mohammedans by the enormous " burden of the confcription. This latter is the " true caufe of the decreafe of the Moham-" medan, and increafe of the Chriftian popu-" lation." And, he adds, " this is the monfter " evil which is gradually confuming the Turkifh " race."

The evidence of Chriftians againft Muffulmans is not admitted in the Kadi Courts, which take the Koran exclufively for their guide ; but in the modern courts, compofed of Medjlis, it is ad-miffible by law. " But it is certain," fays Mifs Irby, who has long refided in Bofnia, "that " in ordinary cafes the evidence of twenty " Chriftians would be outweighed by that of two " Muffulmans."

It would be idle to infist upon the grofs mif-government of the Ottoman Porte. The tefti-mony of every writer of every nation who has examined the fubject, is uniform and decifive, and after reading what they fay, one is tempted to exclaim, in the indignant language of the Roman orator, *Quoufque tandem abutere patientiâ noftrâ?* How long is Chriftian Europe to endure the fpectacle of an alien and infidel government oppreffing Chriftian races?

" Some writers erroneoufly attribute the decay
" of agriculture to the religion or apathy of the
" population; others to the want of roads, of
" hands, of capital, or of practical knowledge.
" Thefe are all only fecondary caufes. The great
" primary caufe is want of fecurity, in other
" words, the defective organifation of Govern-
" ment. A weak, needy, and unftable executive
" is a neceffary caufe of incompetency, cupidity,
" and corruption in the provincial authorities,
" therefore of ruin to agriculture. Of all claffes

" the farmer has moſt need of juſtice, fecurity,
" and encouragement.   Yet here he has to bear
" the whole brunt of taxation—a burden often
" made doubly onerous by the iniquitous mode
" of collection.   Nothing is returned to him in
" the ſhape of roads, police, or juſtice.   His
" produce is taxed over and over again without
" pity."*

In Bulgaria the peaſant is not allowed to remove a ſheaf from the ground before the *multizim*
or farmer of the tithe has felected his portion ;
and in 1869 the harveſt was left all over the
vilayet rotting on the ground, devoured by birds
and vermin.†

The Turk has never aſſimilated with any European people.   There has been no chemical fuſion,
nothing more than mechanical contact.   It is
not only religion but race which keeps him
apart, although in his religion alone we can

---

* Report by Mr. Barron, H.M. Secretary to Embaſſy, on the
Taxation of Turkey.   † Ibid.

fee fufficient caufe for his ifolation. "From
"this oppofition," fays Ranke, "of belief and
"unbelief proceeds the whole political fyftem of
"the Turkifh Empire. The two principles of
"its foundation will always be antagoniftic to
"each other. No hope of forming a united
"nation can confequently be entertained."*

An old Englifh traveller in the reign of
James I., in his "Relation of a Journey begun
in 1610," fays of the ftate of Turkey then:
"We may conclude that the Mahometan reli-
"gion . . . . . wherever it is planted, rooting
"out all virtue, all wifdom and fcience, and in
"fum all liberty and civility and laying the
"earth to wafte, difpeopled and uninhabited,
"neither came from God (fave as a fcourge by
"permiffion) nor can bring them to God that
"follow it." †   I might cite a *catena* of authori-

* Hiftory of Servia, chap. 3.
† Sandys, Relation of a Journey begun A.D. 1610; containing
a Defcription of the Turkifh Empire, &c.

ties all telling the fame melancholy tale, but it is unneceffary, and I will content myfelf with quoting a paffage from an able article in the Edinburgh Review of January 1854, which puts the cafe with brevity and force. "Habits "of toleration and decrees of equality are a dead "letter beyond the diameter of the capital; and "we venture to affirm that more acts of cruelty "and extortion are ftill perpetrated in the "Turkifh Empire than in all thofe countries of "Europe which habitually infpire us with the "ftrongeft commiferation." Even Lord Stratford de Redcliffe, whom no one can accufe of being unfriendly to the Ottoman Porte, has admitted in a letter to the *Times* (January 3, 1876), "that Turkey is weak, fanatical, and "mifgoverned, no one can honeftly deny."

Lord Palmerfton indeed faid in the Houfe of Commons in 1853, "I affert without fear of "contradiction that Turkey, fo far from having "gone back within the laft thirty years, has

" made greater progrefs and improvement, in " every poffible way, than perhaps was ever " made by any other country in the fame " period." No doubt Lord Palmerfton was fincere in his belief, but he miftook profeffion for practice, and trufted to nominal reforms as if they were equivalent to real improvement. It would have puzzled him to make good the affertion if its veracity had been tefted by the actual condition of the people, although he did fpecify " the adminiftration of juftice, the " condition of agriculture, manufactures and " commerce, and religious toleration." Black indeed as midnight muft have been the former condition of Turkey, if an Englifh ftatefman could hail the fainteft twilight as if it were actual funfhine.

In the fame debate Mr. Cobden faid that the Turks in Europe were confidered as intruders ; that their home was Afia ; and the progrefs of events had demonftrated that a Mahommedan

Power could not be maintained in Europe. If he were a Raya fubject of the Porte he fhould fay, " Give me any Chriftian government rather " than a Mahommedan." And furely events have fhown that Mr. Cobden took a jufter view of the queftion than Lord Palmerfton.

What proof is there of even phyfical improvement in the country ? There are roads and roads. But as to the roads in Turkey, a chapter on them might be as fhort as the famous one in Hans Troil's Hiftory of Iceland, which is headed " On the Snakes in Iceland ; " and the whole chapter confifts of the words " There are no fnakes in " Iceland." So there are really " no roads in " Turkey," at leaft none worthy of the name. When I was at Conftantinople in 1869, a new one had been conftructed by an Englifh engineer from Buyukdère on the Bofphorus to the Sultan's Kiofk in the foreft of Belgrade, a diftance of feven or eight miles. He was urged by the Turkifh Government to make the road with the utmoft poffible fpeed, as there was an idea that the Emprefs of the French, whofe vifit was approaching, might poffibly wifh to fee the Kiofk. I was afked by the engineer to accompany him and try the road, but the weather had been wet, and when we reached it, it was in an impaffable ftate of mud. Even between Conftantinople and Adrianople, where the country is a long, wide, undulating plain and the foil clay, the fo-called high road is nothing but a rough track, and a fingle day's rain converts it into flufh and mud. And as to the ftreets of Conftantinople itself they look as if cart-loads of ftones had been dropped from the fky, with deep ruts and holes in them, which no one takes the trouble to fill up.

Corruption has eaten into the heart's core of the Turkifh Government. It was faid of the fall of the Roman Republic, *Nullâ aliâ re magis Romana Refpublica periit, quam quod magiftratûs officia venalia effent.* In Turkey the fale of public offices is the conftant practice, and *viziers* and *pachas* who have bought their posts go to the diftant provinces, and practise every kind of extortion during the fhort and precarious period of their fway.

It ufed to be faid that at all events the Turks were honeft and adhered faithfully to their engagements. But what do the bondholders in England and in France think of this now? The Government has repudiated half of the intereft of its public debt, and the country is in a ftate of financial bankruptcy, the natural confequence of corruption and wafte.

But at laft, in the face of a formidable infurrection, and to fatisfy the demands of indignant Europe, we are promifed a reformation. Old abufes are to be fwept away, and the halcyon reign of equality and juftice is to commence in Turkey. The Sultan has iffued a Firman which breathes the loftieft fentiments of benevolence and good-will to all his fubjects, and we are

aſked to believe that abuſes will be ſwept away
and an era of regeneration will begin. But
who really believes this? At all events the
Firman or *Iradé* is itſelf a proof of the exiſtence
of the evils which it promiſes to redreſs.

It begins with a high-ſounding declaration of
the duty of civilized States to guarantee public
rights, and announces the truiſm that individual
intereſts are only aſſured by the good order and
proſperity of the country generally. Nothing
can be better than the principles it ſets forth
with reſpeſt to the adminiſtration of juſtice, and
the neceſſity of ſeparating the judicial from the
executive office. The judges are to be irremov-
able *ſans cauſe légitime*, and their eleſtion, whether
Muſſulmans or non-Muſſulmans, is to be in the
hands of the people. Some juſt regulations are
made as to taxation, and inequalities are re-
moved. Forced labour is to be aboliſhed. "All
" claſſes of our ſubjeſts who live under the ſhadow
" of our Imperial proteſtion are in our eyes and

"in the fentiments of juftice on the footing of
"complete equality." The public employments and offices are to be open to all, whether
Muffulmans or not. No Raya is to be liable
to a tax for exemption from military fervice
except between the ages of twenty and forty
years. "The greatneſs, the glory, and the
"fecurity of the State can only be maintained
"by the integrity and juftice of the execu-
"tive power, by the obedience of all to the law,
"and by the rigorous obfervation on the part
"of the high and low of the rights of every-
"one."

But have we not heard all this before? If
we refer to the Treaty of Belgrade in 1739
and the Treaty of Siftova in 1791, between
Auftria and the Porte, we find the moft exprefs
ftipulations in favour of the Chriftian fubjects of
the Sultan: "et qu'il ne foit permis à perfonne,
"contre les fufdites capitulations et loix, de
"molefter ou par infulte ou par exaction d'argent

" les dits Religieux et autres, de quelque ordre
" et condition qu'ils foient." * I need not dwell
on the famous *Tanzimaut* which was to have
reformed all Turkey, and which has been con-
feffedly a failure. I will fpeak of what is lefs
known. In the Hatti-Sheriff or Humaîon
of Gulhane iffued by the Sultan in Nov. 1839,
he begins by admitting that " a fucceffion of
" accidents and divers caufes " had brought
about a difregard for the laws, " and the former
" ftrength and profperity have changed into
" weaknefs and poverty "—and declares his
refolve by new inftitutions to give to the
Provinces compofing the Ottoman Empire the
benefit of a good adminiftration. I need not
particularize all the fpecious promifes here made.
It will be enough to ftate that one of them is in
this comprehenfive form. " Thefe Imperial con-
" ceffions fhall extend to all our fubjects, of
" whatever religion or fect they may be ; they

* Wenck, Codex Juris Gentium, vol. i. p. 316 *et feq.*

" shall enjoy them without exception. We there-
" fore grant perfect security to the inhabitants
" of our Empire, in their lives, their honour,
" and their fortunes, as they are secured to
" them by the sacred text of our law."

Again, if we compare the present Hatti-
Sheriff or Firman with the Hatti-Sheriff issued
by the Sultan in 1856 at the close of the
Crimean war, under the pressure of the Great
Powers, we shall find the professions and
promises of the two documents almost identical.
Then the guarantees promised by the Sultan
by the Hatti-Humaîon of Gulhané and the
Tanzimaut to all the subjects of the Empire
" without distinction of classes or religion " were
confirmed and consolidated. Then, as now, all
the privileges and spiritual immunities granted
ab antiquo and at subsequent dates, to all
Christian communities or other non-Mussulman
persuasions established in the Empire were confirmed and maintained. There was to be perfect

toleration of all religions. The adminiſtration of juſtice was to be purified and reformed. Chriſtians were to be admitted into the army, Taxes were to be levied impartially, without diſtinction of claſs or religion. All the ſubjects of the Empire were to be admiſſible to public employments without diſtinction of nationality. The laws againſt corruption and extortion were to be enforced, and ſteps were to be taken for the formation of roads and canals.

But it is unneceſſary to go at length through the catalogue of promiſed reforms. The late Firman is almoſt a copy of its predeceſſors, with a few additions and modifications. But how have the promiſes been kept? The inſurrection in the Herzegovina is a ſufficient anſwer. The very fact of the neceſſity of this new Bill of Rights is in itſelf a confeſſion that the Turkiſh Government, even if it has " kept the word of " promiſe to the ear," has " broken it to the " hope." In other words that paſt promiſes have been nothing but a mockery, a delufion, and a fnare.

But the difficulty of the fituation is very great, and we can hardly be furprifed that Statefmen refponfible for the peace of Europe are obliged to fpeak and act with the utmoft caution and referve.

The jealoufy of the Great Powers, efpecially of Auftria and Ruffia, will never allow any of them to feize the falling fceptre of the Turkifh Sultan. In a Convention between Auftria and the Sublime Porte, which was figned in June 1854, at the outbreak of the Crimean war, the Emperor of Auftria declared that he fully recognifed "that the exiftence of the Ottoman Em-"pire within its prefent limits is neceffary for "the maintenance of the balance of power "between the States of Europe;" and the Convention between Great Britain and France in the month of April the fame year, ftated that "the High Contracting Parties being ani-

"mated with a defire to maintain the balance "of power in Europe," renounced beforehand the acquifition of any advantage for themfelves from the events which might occur.

England, of courfe, with India to guard, could never confent that the Houfe of Romanoff fhould fit on the throne of Conftantinople; and although fhe might fee no danger to her-felf if it was occupied by the Houfe of Hapf-burg, Ruffia is little likely to allow fuch a fplendid prize to fall into the hands of Auftria. French or German occupation is altogether out of the queftion, and the fituation, therefore, of the fucceffion to the dominion of the Ottoman Porte, fuppofing that dominion to come to an end, may be defcribed as fomething like a political dead-lock.

But it is needlefs to fpeculate on the confe-quences of an event which is not likely to happen, or is only amongft the poffibilities of a remote future. The Turks will not quit Europe unlefs they are driven out of Europe, and this could only be at the coft of a war which would fet Europe in a blaze, and the refult of which the moft farfighted ftatefman can neither prophefy nor conjecture. Nor ought we to lay out of fight the terrible mifery which fuch a war would entail upon the population with which we fympathize, and whofe fufferings we wifh to relieve.

But although it is hopelefs to expect that the Ofmanli Turks will crofs the Bofphorus and exchange Conftantinople for Bruffa or fome other city in Afia Minor as their capital, it is by no means chimerical to cherifh the hope that they may be compelled, either by force or from policy, to quit their hold of fome of their outlying provinces, and content themfelves with a much more circumfcribed area.

The Crimea, Greece, Beffarabia, Moldo-Wallachia, Servia, Egypt, have all one after another been torn from their grafp, although to

fome of them they ftill make the idle pretence
of titular fovereignty. For the Slavonic population fouth of the Danube and the Save there
is a Chriftian State already eftablifhed, which
would feem to be the natural nucleus round
which it fhould aggregate. I mean the Principality of Servia. Moldavia and Wallachia were
not long ago as diftinct as Servia and Bofnia, or
Servia and Bulgaria, but they are now blended
together as one independent State—Roumania.

No doubt there are difficulties as regards the
Muffulman population in Bofnia, who have been
ftyled by the Turks in former times, " the lion
" that guarded Stamboul." Some of the Bofnian
Begs are faid to be fanatically jealous of Chriftian
Servia ; but all of them hate the Ofmanli Turks,
and fince the outbreak of infurrection in Herzegovina, the Muffulmans of the Redif, or
referve force, have in many places refufed to
ferve in the army. And Bulgaria alfo has a large
Muffulman element. But if the Chriftian Rayas,

who, in both provinces, greatly exceed the Muſſulmans in number, have been able to live for centuries under Turkiſh rule, there ſeems no reason why the Muſſulmans should not live under Chriſtian rule. I have already mentioned that ſome writers are of opinion that the great bulk of the Boſnian Muſſulmans, whose forefathers were Chriſtians, would not feel much difficulty in returning to their anceſtral faith; but this I myſelf do not believe. They would, however, appreciate the bleſſings of good government, and would thankfully ſee themſelves freed from the oppreſſion and extortion of Pachas ſent from Conſtantinople to ſqueeze a fortune out of the people, whether Muſſulmans or Chriſtians.

Turkey, in faƈt, is in this poſition : If left to herſelf ſhe will periſh, not ſlowly, but rapidly from internal decay. If propped up by foreign influence, and held in a ſtate of tutelage, ſhe will loſe—indeed ſhe has already loſt—all real ſenſe of independence, and her ſubjeƈts will ceaſe to refpect a Government kept in leading-ftrings by ftrangers and aliens. And after all, what can we expect from meddling and interference? We may advife, we may lecture as we will, but

" *Naturam expellas furcâ, tamen ufque recurret.*"

The Sultan and his Minifters at Conftantinople may make what promifes they pleafe, but what effect will thefe have upon the obfcure fufferings of the poor Rayas in Bofnia and Bulgaria? The experience of centuries has fhown that the Ofmanli Turks are not fit to govern Chriftian communities, and the fooner the Great Powers can agree together to emancipate them even by force, without a convulfion which would open the door to Ruffian ambition, the better will it be for millions of the human race. Why fhould not there be guaranteed to Bofnia and Bulgaria an autonomy like that which has already been granted to Servia and Roumania? If the Great Powers could agree in this, the Sultan would have no alternative but to grant it, for the Ottoman Porte could not cope with any one of them in arms, and muſt perforce yield to their collective demand. At all events Herzegovina, which is ſeparated from Boſnia proper by a barrier of mountains, might be given to Montenegro. The ſympathies of the inhabitants of both countries are in uniſon ; they are both Chriſtian ; they both ſeem deſigned by Nature to form one territory ; and ſo long as Herzegovina belongs to Turkey, diſcontent will lead to inſurrection, and all the diplomacy of Europe will not prevent the Montenegrins from ſecretly aſſiſting her attempts to throw off the burden of the Turkiſh yoke.

This may be called a diſmemberment of the Empire ; and ſo it is. But I believe that it would be better for even Turkey herſelf to quit her hold of the Danubian Provinces, and confine herſelf to Roumelia and Albania. The road to Conſtantinople is as open through Servia as through Bofnia, and Servia fhe has already loft. She would have the Balkan for her northern frontier, and as regards Roumelia, the population confifts chiefly of Ofmanli Turks, with whofe internal condition we need not concern ourfelves. And for them this limited area would be fufficient. They are decreafing in numbers from phyfical and focial caufes, which it is unneceffary to particularize, and every writer on Turkey attefts the gradual decay of the Ofmanli population.

Nobody pretends that the poffeffion of Bofnia and Bulgaria would enable the Ottoman Porte, unaided, to refift an invafion by either Ruffia or Auftria, and therefore as againft foreign aggreffion, thofe provinces are practically worthlefs. And in the meantime they are, or at all events Bofnia is, a fource of weaknefs, as a difcontented and fuffering population muft always be.

Lord Chatham once exclaimed in the Houfe of Lords, " I rejoice that America has refifted! "

And there are few Englishmen who would not each say in his heart, " I rejoice that Herzego- " vina has resisted ! " It is impossible not to feel the warmest sympathy with the efforts of a long down-trodden people to free themselves from the yoke of oppression ; and if they succeed in the struggle, all Christendom will hail their deliverance with joy. But they have to fight against fearful odds, when the whole military strength of the Ottoman Empire is employed to crush them. It is difficult to believe that if left to themselves they will be able to resist the overwhelming force that can be brought against them. Any active assistance given by Montenegro or Servia would probably be stopped by the action of the Great Powers, who are not likely to allow those States to interfere in a quarrel between the Porte and its subjects, from which they themselves, so far as military action is concerned, stand aloof. And as to interference in any shape by those Powers who were signataries to the Treaty of Paris in 1856 to which the Sultan was a party, it may be a queftion whether it is not an actual breach of one of the exprefs ftipulations of that Treaty; for, after acknowledging " the high value of the com- " munication " of the Firman which the Sultan had juft iffued for ameliorating the condition of his fubjects " without diftinction of religion or " of race," the Treaty goes on to fay, " It is " clearly underftood that it cannot *in any cafe* " give to the faid Powers the right to interfere, " either collectively or feparately, in the relations " of His Majefty the Sultan with his fubjects, " nor in the internal adminiftration of his " Empire." It may, however, be anfwered that *neceffitas non habet legem*—and when all agree to interfere, the neceffity feems proved.

But whatever courfe Governments may take, one thing is clear. Individuals have no right to promote or fofter civil war in the territories of a Power with whom their own country is at

peace. They may fympathife with the infurgents, but they cannot, without violating the
rules of international law, and without a breach
of their own municipal law, render them active
affiftance. To combine together for the purpofe
of contributing funds in aid of a revolt in a
foreign kingdom with which we are not at war,
is a punifhable mifdemeanor at common law;
and I would recommend to the ferious attention of thofe who wifh to fubfcribe money to
help the infurgents in Herzegovina the weighty
words of Lord Lyndhurft, who faid in the
Houfe of Lords on the 4th of March, 1853,—

" If a number of Britifh fubjects were to
" combine and confpire together to excite revolt
" among the inhabitants of a friendly State—of
" a State united in alliance with us—and thefe
" perfons, in purfuance of that confpiracy, were
" to iffue manifeftoes and proclamations for the
" purpofe of carrying that object into effect ;
" above all, *if they were to fubfcribe money for*

" *the purpofe of purchafing arms* to give effect to
" that intended enterprife, I conceive, and I ftate
" with confidence, that each perfon would be
" guilty of a mifdemeanor, and liable to fuffer
" punifhment by the laws of this country, inaf-
" much as their conduct would tend to embroil
" the two countries together, to lead to remon-
" ftrances by the one with the other, and ulti-
" mately, it might be, to war. . . . The offence
" of endeavouring to excite revolt among the
" fubjects of a neighbouring State, is an offence
" againft the Law of Nations. No writer on
" the Law of Nations ftates otherwife. But
" the Law of Nations, according to the decifions
" of our greateft Judges, is part of the law of
" England."

It may feem cold and ungenerous to be ready
with our fympathy, but refufe all active aid to a
people ftruggling to be free. But our duty as
citizens is clear. So long as England is at peace
with Turkey—no fubject of the Queen is juftified

in affifting, by arms or money, a revolt againft the fovereign authority of the Ottoman Porte. So long as her Empire is tolerated in Europe and fhe exifts as an independent State with which we have treaties and diplomatic inter-courfe, we cannot releafe ourfelves from the duties impofed upon us by the *jus gentium* and the law of our own country. For although, to quote the words of a great authority on the Law of Nations—Wheaton : " the relations which " have prevailed between the Ottoman Empire " and the other European States, have only " recently brought the former within the pale " of that public law by which the latter are " governed,"—yet as fhe has been fo brought within the pale, fhe muft be treated accordingly. But the rule of conduct due from individuals in this cafe need not be the rule of Governments, and as they have before interfered to fave Turkey from the aggreffion of the Pacha of Egypt, they might (unlefs pofitive treaty prevents them) interfere to fave the Chriftian provinces of Turkey from oppreffion and mif-rule. And this might be done, if not on the high ground of humanity, which is perhaps a dangerous plea for armed intervention, yet on the ground of felf-defence. For

> . . . *tua res agitur cum proximus ardet*
> *Ucalegon.*

And neither Ruffia nor Auftria can confider the courfe which a Slavonic infurrection may take as one in which they have not the deepeft concern. Happily, the ftate of public opinion in Europe is now generally favourable to fome kind of intervention, and we may hope that it will be of fuch a kind as will be effectual to put a ftop to the grofs and crying abufes of which the Slavonic Provinces of Turkey have been the theatre. But if that fails—and I confefs I have not much faith in its fuccefs, for paft experience almoft forbids hope—then we may further hope that the more decifive ftep will be taken of freeing altogether thofe Provinces from the grafp of the Ottoman Porte, and placing them, like Belgium, under a collective guarantee of neutrality. Such a policy might, perhaps, be the beft even now, for fuch, I believe, muft ultimately be the refult. And it will be the happieft refult. For few will be difpofed to agree with the opinion of the late Fuad Pacha in his Political Teftament, addreffed from his dying bed to the Sultan, and expreffing the Turkifh point of view. "But a Montenegro, a principality of "Servia, a kingdom of Armenia, without con- "ferring the flighteft advantage either upon "themfelves or the world, can never be anything "further than ftates more or lefs chimerical, "wretched fragments of former convulfions of "humanity, inevitably a prey to any new con- "queror, prejudicial to the progrefs of mankind, "and dangerous for the peace of the world." *

* Quoted by Farley, Decline of Turkey. London: 1875. A remarkable pamphlet, well worth ftudying.

There is far more danger in keeping difcontented Provinces to fefter in the midft of a decaying State, and the progrefs of mankind is beft fecured by the poffeffion of free inftitutions.

I will conclude with the words fpoken by the prefent Foreign Secretary not twelve years ago, in which I heartily agree :—

"I believe the queftion of the breaking up of "the Turkifh Empire to be only a queftion of "time, and probably not a very long time. "The Turks have played their part in hiftory; "they have had their day, and that day is over ; "and I do not underftand, except it be from the "influence of old diplomatic traditions, the "determination of our older ftatefmen to ftand "by the Turkifh rule, whether right or wrong. "*I think we are making for ourfelves enemies of* "*races, which will very foon become, in Eaftern* "*Europe, dominant races ;* and I think we are "keeping back countries by whofe improve- "ment we, as the grea' traders of the world,

" fhould be the great gainers, and that we are
" doing this for no earthly advantage, either
" prefent or profpective." *

* Lord Stanley's fpeech at King's Lynn, October, 1864.

THE END.

50A, ALDEMARLE STREET, LONDON,
January, 1876.

MR. MURRAY'S

GENERAL LIST OF WORKS.

ALBERT (The) MEMORIAL. A Descriptive and Illustrated
Account of the National Monument erected to the PRINCE CONSORT
at Kensington. Illustrated by Engravings of its Architecture, Decora-
tions, Sculptured Groups, Statues, Mosaics, Metalwork, &c. With
Descriptive Text. By DOYNE C. BELL. With 24 Plates. Folio. 12*l.* 12*s.*

———— (PRINCE) SPEECHES AND ADDRESSES with an Introduction, giving some outline of his Character. With Portrait. 8vo.
10*s.* 6*d.*; or *Popular Edition*, fcap. 8vo. 1*s.*

ALBERT DURER; his Life and Works. By DR. THAUSING,
Keeper of Archduke Albert's Art Collection at Vienna. Translated
from the German. With Portrait Illustrations. Medium 8vo.
[*In the Press.*

ABBOTT'S (REV. J.) Memoirs of a Church of England Missionary
in the North American Colonies. Post 8vo. 2*s.*

ABERCROMBIE'S (JOHN) Enquiries concerning the Intellectual
Powers and the Investigation of Truth. Fcap. 8vo. 3*s.* 6*d.*

———————————— Philosophy of the Moral Feelings. Fcap. 8vo.
2*s.* 6*d.*

ACLAND'S (REV. CHARLES) Popular Account of the Manners and
Customs of India. Post 8vo. 2*s.*

ÆSOP'S FABLES. A New Version. With Historical Preface.
By Rev. THOMAS JAMES. With 100 Woodcuts, by TENNIEL and WOLF.
Post 8vo. 2*s.* 6*d.*

AGRICULTURAL (ROYAL) JOURNAL. (*Published half yearly.*)

AIDS TO FAITH: a Series of Theological Essays. 8vo. 9*s.*

CONTENTS.

Miracles	DEAN MANSEL.
Evidences of Christianity	BISHOP FITZGERALD.
Prophecy & Mosaic Record of Creation	DR. McCAUL.
Ideology and Subscription	Canon COOK.
The Pentateuch	Canon RAWLINSON.
Inspiration	BISHOP HAROLD BROWNE.
Death of Christ	ARCHBISHOP THOMSON.
Scripture and its Interpretation	BISHOP ELLICOTT.

AMBER-WITCH (THE). A most interesting Trial for Witchcraft. Translated by LADY DUFF GORDON. Post 8vo. 2*s.*

ARMY LIST (THE). *Published Monthly by Authority.*

ARTHUR'S (LITTLE) History of England. By LADY CALLCOTT.
New Edition, continued to 1872. With 36 Woodcuts. Fcap. 8vo. 1*s.* 6*d.*

AUSTIN'S (JOHN) LECTURES ON GENERAL JURISPRUDENCE; or, the
Philosophy of Positive Law. Edited by ROBERT CAMPBELL. 2 Vols.
8vo. 32*s.*

———————— STUDENT'S EDITION, compiled from the above work.
Post 8vo. 12*s.*

ARNOLD'S (THOS.) Ecclesiastical and Secular Architecture of
Scotland: The Abbeys, Churches, Castles, and Mansions. With Illustrations. Medium 8vo. [*In Preparation.*

B

ADMIRALTY PUBLICATIONS; Issued by direction of the Lords
Commissioners of the Admiralty:—

A MANUAL OF SCIENTIFIC ENQUIRY, for the Use of Travellers.
Fourth Edition. Edited by ROBERT MAIN, M.A. Woodcuts. Post
8vo. 3s. 6d.

GREENWICH ASTRONOMICAL OBSERVATIONS 1841 to 1846,
and 1847 to 1871. Royal 4to. 20s. each.

MAGNETICAL AND METEOROLOGICAL OBSERVATIONS. 1840
to 1847. Royal 4to. 20s. each.

APPENDICES TO OBSERVATIONS.
   1837. Logarithms of Sines and Cosines in Time. 3s.
   1842. Catalogue of 1439 Stars, from Observations made in 1836 to
         1841. 4s.
   1845. Longitude of Valentia (Chronometrical). 3s.
   1847. Description of Altazimuth. 3s.
         Twelve Years' Catalogue of Stars, from Observations made
         in 1836 to 1847. 4s.
         Description of Photographic Apparatus. 2s.
   1851. Maskelyne's Ledger of Stars. 3s.
   1852. I. Description of the Transit Circle. 3s.
   1853. Refraction Tables. 3s.
   1854. Description of the Zenith Tube. 3s.
         Six Years' Catalogue of Stars, from Observations. 1848 to
         1853. 4s.
   1862. Seven Years' Catalogue of Stars, from Observations. 1854 to
         1860. 10s.
         Plan of Ground Buildings. 3s.
         Longitude of Valentia (Galvanic). 2s.
   1864. Moon's Semid. from Occultations. 2s.
         Planetary Observations, 1831 to 1835. 2s.
   1868. Corrections of Elements of Jupiter and Saturn. 2s.
         Second Seven Years' Catalogue of 2760 Stars for 1861 to
         1867. 4s.
         Description of the Great Equatorial. 3s.
   1856. Descriptive Chronograph. 3s.
   1860. Reduction of Deep Thermometer Observations. 2s.
   1871. History and Description of Water Telescope. 3s.

   Cape of Good Hope Observations (Star Ledgers). 1856 to 1863. 2s.
   ——   ——   —— 1856. 5s.
   ——————— Astronomical Results. 1857 to 1858. 5s.
   Report on Teneriffe Astronomical Experiment. 1856. 5s.
   Paramatta Catalogue of 7385 Stars. 1822 to 1826. 4s.

ASTRONOMICAL RESULTS. 1847 to 1871. 4to. 3s. each.

MAGNETICAL AND METEOROLOGICAL RESULTS. 1847 to
   1871. 4to. 3s. each.

REDUCTION OF THE OBSERVATIONS OF PLANETS. 1750 to
   1830. Royal 4to. 20s. each.

——————————————— LUNAR OBSERVATIONS. 1750
   to 1830. 2 Vols. Royal 4to. 20s. each.

——————————— 1831 to 1851. 4to. 10s. each.

BERNOULLI'S SEXCENTENARY TABLE. 1779. 4to. 5s.

BESSEL'S AUXILIARY TABLES FOR HIS METHOD OF CLEAR-
   ING LUNAR DISTANCES. 8vo. 2s.

ENCKE'S BERLINER JAHRBUCH, for 1830. *Berlin*, 1828. 8vo. 9s.

HANSEN'S TABLES DE LA LUNE. 4to. 20s.

LAX'S TABLES FOR FINDING THE LATITUDE AND LONGI-
   TUDE. 1821. 8vo. 10s.

ADMIRALTY PUBLICATIONS—*continued.*

LUNAR OBSERVATIONS at GREENWICH. 1783 to 1819. Compared with the Tables, 1821. 4to. 7s. 6d.

MACLEAR ON LACAILLE'S ARC OF MERIDIAN. 2 Vols. 20s. each.

MAYER'S DISTANCES of the MOON'S CENTRE from the PLANETS. 1822, 3s.; 1823, 4s. 6d. 1824 to 1835. 8vo. 4s. each.

———— TABULÆ MOTUUM SOLIS ET LUNÆ. 1770. 5s.

———— ASTRONOMICAL OBSERVATIONS MADE AT GOTTINGEN, from 1756 to 1761. 1826. Folio. 7s. 6d.

NAUTICAL ALMANACS, from 1767 to 1877. 2s. 6d. each.

———— ——— SELECTIONS FROM, up to 1812. 8vo. 5s. 1834-54. 5s.

———— ——— SUPPLEMENTS, 1828 to 1833, 1837 and 1838. 2s. each.

———— ——— TABLE requisite to be used with the N.A. 1781. 8vo. 5s.

SABINE'S PENDULUM EXPERIMENTS to DETERMINE THE FIGURE OF THE EARTH. 1825. 4to. 40s.

SHEPHERD'S TABLES for CORRECTING LUNAR DISTANCES. 1772. Royal 4to. 21s.

———— ——— TABLES, GENERAL, of the MOON'S DISTANCE from the SUN, and 10 STARS. 1787. Folio. 5s. 6d.

TAYLOR'S SEXAGESIMAL TABLE. 1780. 4to. 15s.

———— TABLES OF LOGARITHMS. 4to. 60s.

TIARK'S ASTRONOMICAL OBSERVATIONS for the LONGITUDE of MADEIRA. 1822. 4to. 5s.

———— CHRONOMETRICAL OBSERVATIONS for DIFFERENCES of LONGITUDE between DOVER, PORTSMOUTH, and FALMOUTH. 1823. 4to. 5s.

VENUS and JUPITER: OBSERVATIONS of, compared with the TABLES. London, 1822. 4to. 2s.

WALES' AND BAYLY'S ASTRONOMICAL OBSERVATIONS. 1777. 4to. 21s.

———— REDUCTION OF ASTRONOMICAL OBSERVATIONS MADE IN THE SOUTHERN HEMISPHERE. 1764—1771. 1788. 4to. 10s. 6d.

BARBAULD'S (MRS.) Hymns in Prose for Children. With Illustrations. Crown 8vo. 5s.

BARROW'S (SIR JOHN) Autobiographical Memoir, from Early Life to Advanced Age. Portrait. 8vo. 16s.

———— (JOHN) Life, Exploits, and Voyages of Sir Francis Drake. Post 8vo. 2s.

BARRY'S (SIR CHARLES) Life and Works. By CANON BARRY. With Portrait and Illustrations. Medium 8vo. 15s.

BATES' (H. W.) Records of a Naturalist on the River Amazon during eleven years of Adventure and Travel. Illustrations. Post 8vo. 7s. 6d.

BAX'S (CAPTAIN) Russian Tartary, Eastern Siberia, China, Japan, and Formosa. A Narrative of a Cruise in the Eastern Seas. With Map and Illustrations. Crown 8vo. 12s.

BEAUCLERK'S (LADY DIANA) Summer and Winter in Norway. With Illustrations. Small 8vo. 6s.

BELCHER'S (LADY) Account of the Mutineers of the 'Bounty,' and their Descendants; with their Settlements in Pitcairn and Norfolk Islands. With Illustrations. Post 8vo. 12s.

BELL'S (SIR CHAS.) Familiar Letters. Portrait. Post 8vo. 12s.

BELT'S (Thos.) Naturalist in Nicaragua, including a Residence at the Gold Mines of Chontales; with Journeys in the Savannahs
and Forests; and Observations on Animals and Plants. Illustrations.
Post 8vo. 12s.

BERTRAM'S (Jas. G.) Harvest of the Sea: an Account of British
Food Fishes, including sketches of Fisheries and Fisher Folk. With
50 Illustrations. 8vo. 9s.

BIBLE COMMENTARY. Explanatory and Critical. With
a Revision of the Translation. By Bishops and Clergy of the
ANGLICAN CHURCH. Edited by F. C. Cook, M.A., Canon of Exeter.
Medium 8vo. Vol. I., 30s. Vols. II. and III., 36s. Vol. IV, 24s.
Vol. V., 20s. Vol. VI., 20s.

Vol. I.	Genesis. Exodus. Leviticus. Numbers. Deuteronomy.	Vol. IV.	Job. Psalms. Proverbs. Ecclesiastes. Song of Solomon.
Vols. II. and III.	Joshua. Judges, Ruth, Samuel. Kings, Chronicles, Ez- ra, Nehemiah, Esther.	Vol. V.	Isaiah. Jeremiah.
		Vol. VI.	Ezekiel. Daniel. Minor Prophets.

BIRCH'S (Samuel) History of Ancient Pottery and Porcelain:
Egyptian, Assyrian, Greek, Roman, and Etruscan. With Coloured
Plates and 200 Illustrations. Medium 8vo. 42s.

BIRD'S (Isabella) Hawaiian Archipelago; or Six Months Among
the Palm Groves, Coral Reefs, and Volcanoes of the Sandwich Islands.
With Illustrations. Crown 8vo. 12s.

BISSET'S (Andrew) History of the Commonwealth of England,
from the Death of Charles I. to the Expulsion of the Long Parliament
by Cromwell. Chiefly from the MSS. in the State Paper Office. 2 vols.
8vo. 30s.

——— (General) Sport and War in South Africa from 1834
to 1867, with a Narrative of the Duke of Edinburgh's Visit. With
Map and Illustrations. Crown 8vo. 14s.

BLACKSTONE'S COMMENTARIES: adapted to the Present
State of the Law. By R. Malcolm Kerr, LL.D. Revised Edition,
incorporating all the Recent Changes in the Law. 4 vols. 8vo.

BLUNT'S (Rev. J. J.) Undesigned Coincidences in the Writings of
the Old and New Testaments, an Argument of their Veracity: containing
the Books of Moses, Historical and Prophetical Scriptures, and the
Gospels and Acts. Post 8vo. 6s.

——— History of the Church in the First Three Centuries.
Post 8vo. 6s.

——— ——— Parish Priest; His Duties, Acquirements and Obliga-
tions. Post 8vo. 6s.

——— Lectures on the Right Use of the Early Fathers.
8vo. 9s.

——— University Sermons. Post 8vo. 6s.

——— Plain Sermons. 2 vols. Post 8vo. 12s.

BLOMFIELD'S (Bishop) Memoir, with Selections from his Correspondence. By his Son. Portrait, post 8vo. 12s.

BOSWELL'S (James) Life of Samuel Johnson, LL.D. Including
the Tour to the Hebrides. By Mr. Croker. New Edition. Portraits.
4 vols. 8vo.   [In Preparation.

BRACE'S (C. L.) Manual of Ethnology; or the Races of the Old
World. Post 8vo. 6s.

BOOK OF COMMON PRAYER. Illustrated with Coloured
Borders, Initial Letters, and Woodcuts. 8vo. 18s.

BORROW'S (George) Bible in Spain; or the Journeys, Adventures, and Imprisonments of an Englishman in an Attempt to circulate the Scriptures in the Peninsula. Post 8vo. 5s.

———— Gypsies of Spain; their Manners, Customs, Religion, and Language. With Portrait. Post 8vo. 5s.

———— Lavengro ; The Scholar—The Gypsy—and the Priest. Post 8vo. 5s.

———— Romany Rye—a Sequel to "Lavengro." Post 8vo. 5s.

———— Wild Wales : its People, Language, and Scenery. Post 8vo. 5s.

———— Romano Lavo-Lil; Word-Book of the Romany, or English Gypsy Language; with Specimens of their Poetry, and an account of certain Gypsyries. Post 8vo. 10s. 6d.

BRAY'S (Mrs.) Life of Thomas Stothard, R.A. With Portrait and 60 Woodcuts. 4to. 21s.

———— Revolt of the Protestants in the Cevennes. With some Account of the Huguenots in the Seventeenth Century. Post 8vo. 10s. 6d.

BRITISH ASSOCIATION REPORTS. 8vo.

York and Oxford, 1831-32, 13s. 6d.	Liverpool, 1854, 18s.
Cambridge, 1833, 12s.	Glasgow, 1855, 15s.
Edinburgh, 1834, 15s.	Cheltenham, 1856, 18s.
Dublin, 1835, 13s. 6d.	Dublin, 1857, 15s.
Bristol, 1836, 12s.	Leeds, 1838, 20s.
Liverpool, 1837, 16s. 6d.	Aberdeen, 1859, 15s.
Newcastle, 1838, 15s.	Oxford, 1860, 25s.
Birmingham, 1839, 13s. 6d.	Manchester, 1861, 15s.
Glasgow, 1840, 15s.	Cambridge, 1862, 20s.
Plymouth, 1841, 13s. 6d.	Newcastle, 1863, 25s.
Manchester, 1842, 10s. 6d.	Bath, 1864, 18s.
Cork, 1843, 12s.	Birmingham, 1865, 25s.
York, 1844, 20s.	Nottingham, 1866, 24s.
Cambridge, 1845, 12s.	Dundee, 1967, 26s.
Southampton, 1846, 15s.	Norwich, 1868, 25s.
Oxford, 1847, 18s.	Exeter, 1869, 22s.
Swansea, 1848, 9s.	Liverpool, 1870, 18s.
Birmingham, 1849, 10s.	Edinburgh, 1871, 16s.
Edinburgh, 1850, 15s.	Brighton, 1872, 24s.
Ipswich, 1851, 16s. 6d.	Bradford, 1873, 25s.
Belfast, 1852, 15s.	Belfast, 1974.
Hull, 1853, 10s. 6d.	

BROUGHTON'S (Lord) Journey through Albania, Turkey in Europe and Asia, to Constantinople. Illustrations. 2 Vols. 8vo. 30s.

———— Visits to Italy. 2 Vols. Post 8vo. 18s.

BROWNLOW'S (Lady) Reminiscences of a Septuagenarian. From the year 1802 to 1815 Post 8vo. 7s. 6d.

BRUGSCH'S (Professor) History of Ancient Egypt. Derived from Monuments and Inscriptions. New Edition. Translated by H. Danby Seymour. 8vo. [In Preparation.

BUCKLEY'S (Arabella B.) Short History of Natural Science, and the Progress of Discovery from the time of the Greeks to the present day, for Schools and young Persons. Illustrations. Post 8vo. 9s.

BURGON'S (Rev. J. W.) Christian Gentleman; or, Memoir of Patrick Fraser Tytler. Post 8vo. 9s.

———— Letters from Rome. Post 8vo. 12s.

BURN'S (Col.) Dictionary of Naval and Military Technical Terms, English and French—French and English. Crown 8vo. 15s.

BURROW'S (Montagu) Constitutional Progress. A Series of Lectures delivered before the University of Oxford. Post 8vo. 5s.

BUXTON'S (CHARLES) Memoirs of Sir Thomas Fowell Buxton, Bart. With Selections from his Correspondence. Portrait. 8vo. 16s. *Popular Edition.* Fcap. 8vo. 5s.

———— Notes of Thought. With Biographical Sketch. By Rev. LLEWELLYN DAVIES. With Portrait. Crown 8vo. 10s. 6d.

BURCKHARDT'S (DR. JACOB) Cicerone ; or Art Guide to Paint-ing in Italy. Edited by REV. DR. A. VON ZAHN, and Translated from the German by MRS. A. CLOUGH. Post 8vo. 6s.

BYLES' (SIR JOHN) Foundations of Religion in the Mind and Heart of Man. Post 8vo. 6s.

BYRON'S (LORD) Life, Letters, and Journals. By THOMAS MOORE. *Cabinet Edition.* Plates. 6 Vols. Fcap. 8vo. 18s.; or One Volume, Portraits. Royal 8vo., 7s. 6d.

———————— and Poetical Works. *Popular Edition.* Portraits. 2 vols. Royal 8vo. 15s.

—— Poetical Works. *Library Edition.* Portrait. 6 Vols. 8vo. 45s.

-          *Cabinet Edition.* Plates. 10 Vols. 12mo. 30s.

————————   *Pocket Edition.* 8 Vols. 24mo. 21s. *In a case.*

———————— *Popular Edition.* Plates. Royal 8vo. 7s. 6d.

            Pearl Edition. Crown 8vo. 2s. 6d.

———————— Childe Harold. With 80 Engravings. Crown 8vo. 12s.

——   - ——————— 16mo. 2s. 6d.

———————— . Vignettes. 16mo. 1s.

- ———————————- Portrait. 16mo. 6d.

————   - Tales and Poems. 24mo. 2s. 6d.

     - Miscellaneous. 2 Vols. 24mo. 5s.

        Dramas and Plays. 2 Vols. 24mo. 5s.

——   —— Don Juan and Beppo. 2 Vols. 24mo. 5s.

· ———— Beauties. Poetry and Prose. Portrait. Fcap. 8vo. 3s. 6d.

BUTTMAN'S Lexilogus ; a Critical Examination of the Meaning of numerous Greek Words, chiefly in Homer and Hesiod. By Rev. J. R. FISHLAKE. 8vo. 12s.

———— Irregular Greek Verbs. With all the Tenses extant—their Formation, Meaning, and Usage, with Notes, by Rev. J. R. FISHLAKE. Post 8vo. 6s.

CALLCOTT'S (LADY) Little Arthur's History of England. *New Edition, brought down to* 1872. With Woodcuts. Fcap. 8vo. 1s. 6d.

CARNARVON'S (LORD) Portugal, Gallicia, and the Basque Provinces. Post 8vo. 3s. 6d.

———————— Reminiscences of Athens and the Morea. With Map. Crown 8vo. 7s. 6d.

——— - - Recollections of the Druses of Lebanon. With Notes on their Religion. Post 8vo. 5s. 6d.

CASTLEREAGH (THE) DESPATCHES, from the commencement of the official career of Viscount Castlereagh to the close of his life. 12 Vols. 8vo. 14s. each.

CAMPBELL'S (LORD) Lord Chancellors and Keepers of the Great Seal of England. From the Earliest Times to the Death of Lord Eldon in 1838. 10 Vols. Crown 8vo. 6s. each.

———— Chief Justices of England. From the Norman Conquest to the Death of Lord Tenterden. 4 Vols. Crown 8vo. 6s. each.

———— Lords Lyndhurst and Brougham. 8vo. 16s.

———— Shakspeare's Legal Acquirements. 8vo. 5s. 6d.

———— Lord Bacon. Fcap. 8vo. 2s. 6d.

———— (SIR NEIL) Account of Napoleon at Fontainebleau and Elba. Being a Journal of Occurrences and Notes of his Conversations, &c. Portrait. 8vo. 15s.

———— (SIR GEORGE) India as it may be: an Outline of a proposed Government and Policy. 8vo.

———— (THOS.) Essay on English Poetry. With Short Lives of the British Poets. Post 8vo. 3s. 6d.

CATHCART'S (SIR GEORGE) Commentaries on the War in Russia and Germany, 1812-13. Plans. 8vo. 14s.

CAVALCASELLE AND CROWE'S History of Painting in NORTH ITALY, from the 14th to the 16th Century. With Illustrations. 2 Vols. 8vo. 42s.

———— Early Flemish Painters, their Lives and Works. Illustrations. Post 8vo. 10s. 6d.; or Large Paper, 8vo. 15s.

CHILD'S (G. CHAPLIN, M.D.) Benedicite; or, Song of the Three Children; being Illustrations of the Power, Beneficence, and Design manifested by the Creator in his works. Post 8vo. 6s.

CHISHOLM'S (Mrs.) Perils of the Polar Seas; True Stories of Arctic Discovery and Adventure. Illustrations. Post 8vo. 6s.

CHURTON'S (ARCHDEACON) Gongora. An Historical Essay on the Age of Philip III. and IV. of Spain. With Translations. Portrait. 2 Vols. Small 8vo. 12s.

———— Poetical Remains, Translations and Imitations. Portrait. Post 8vo. 7s. 6d.

———— New Testament. Edited with a Plain Practical Commentary for Families and General Readers. With 100 Panoramic and other Views, from Sketches made on the Spot. 2 vols. 8vo. 2s.

CICERO'S LIFE AND TIMES. His Character as a Statesman, Orator, and Friend, with a Selection from his Correspondence and Orations. By WILLIAM FORSYTH, M.P. With Illustrations. 8vo. 10s. 6d.

CLARK'S (SIR JAMES) Memoir of Dr. John Conolly. Comprising a Sketch of the Treatment of the Insane in Europe and America. With Portrait. Post 8vo. 10s. 6d.

CLIVE'S (LORD) Life. By REV. G. R. GLEIG. Post 8vo. 3s. 6d.

CLODE'S (C. M.) Military Forces of the Crown; their Administration and Government. 2 Vols. 8vo. 21s. each.

———— Administration of Justice under Military and Martial Law, as applicable to the Army, Navy, Marine, and Auxiliary Forces. 8vo. 12s.

COLCHESTER (THE) Papers. The Diary and Correspondence of Charles Abbott, Lord Colchester, Speaker of the House of Commons, 1802-1817. Portrait. 3 Vols. 8vo. 42s.

CHURCH (The) & THE AGE. Essays on the Principles and Present Position of the Anglican Church. 2 vols. 8vo. 26s. Contents:—

VOL. I.

Anglican Principles.—Dean Hook.
Modern Religious Thought.—Bishop Ellicott.
State, Church, and Synods.—Rev. Dr. Irons.
Religious Use of Taste.—Rev. R. St. John Tyrwhitt.
Place of the Laity.—Professor Burrows.
Parish Priest.—Rev. Walsham How.
Divines of 16th and 17th Centuries. —Rev. A. W. Haddan.
Liturgies and Ritual, Rev. M. F. Sadler.
Church & Education.—Canon Barry.
Indian Missions.— Sir Bartle Frere.
Church and the People.—Rev. W. D. Maclagan.
Conciliation and Comprehension.— Rev. Dr. Weir.

VOL. II.

Church and Pauperism.—Earl Nelson.
American Church.—Bishop of Western New York.
Church and Science. — Prebendary Clark.
Ecclesiastical Law.—Isambard Brunel.
Church & National Education.— Canon Norris.
Church and Universities.—John G. Talbot.
Toleration.—Dean Cowie.
Eastern Church and Anglican Communion.—Rev. Geo. Williams.
A Disestablished Church.—Dean of Cashel.
Christian Tradition.—Rev. Dr. Irons.
Dogma.—Rev. Dr. Weir.
Parochial Councils. — Archdeacon Chapman.

COLERIDGE'S (Samuel Taylor) Table-Talk. Portrait. 12mo. 3s. 6d.

COLLINGWOOD'S (Cuthbert) Rambles of a Naturalist on the Shores and Waters of the China Sea. With Illustrations. 8vo. 16s.

COLONIAL LIBRARY. [See Home and Colonial Library.]

COOK'S (Canon) Sermons Preached at Lincoln's Inn. 8vo. 9s.

COOKE'S (E. W.) Artist's Portfolio. Being Sketches made during Tours in Holland, Germany, Italy, Egypt, &c. 60 Plates. Royal 4to. [In Preparation.

COOKERY (Modern Domestic). Founded on Principles of Economy and Practical Knowledge, By a Lady. Woodcuts. Fcap. 8vo. 5s.

COOPER'S (T. T.) Travels of a Pioneer of Commerce on an Overland Journey from China towards India. Illustrations. 8vo. 16s.

CORNWALLIS (The) Papers and Correspondence during the American War,—Administrations in India,—Union with Ireland, and Peace of Amiens. 3 Vols. 8vo. 63s.

COWPER'S (Countess) Diary while Lady of the Bedchamber to Caroline, Princess of Wales, 1714—20. Portrait. 8vo. 10s. 6d.

CRABBE'S (Rev. George) Life and Poetical Works. With Illustrations. Royal 8vo. 7s.

CRAWFORD & BALCARRE'S (Earl of) Etruscan Inscriptions. Analyzed, Translated, and Commented upon. 8vo. 12s.

——————— Argo ; or the Quest of the Golden Fleece. In Ten Books. 8vo.

CROKER'S (J. W.) Progressive Geography for Children. 18mo. 1s. 6d.

——————— Stories for Children, Selected from the History of England. Woodcuts. 16mo. 2s. 6d.

——————— Boswell's Life of Johnson. Including the Tour to the Hebrides. *New Edition.* Portraits. 4 vols. 8vo. [In Preparation.

——————— Early Period of the French Revolution. 8vo. 15s.

——————— Historical Essay on the Guillotine. Fcap. 8vo. 1s.

CUMMING'S (R. Gordon) Five Years of a Hunter's Life in the Far Interior of South Africa. Woodcuts. Post 8vo. 6s.

CROWE'S AND CAVALCASELLE'S Lives of the Early Flemish Painters. Woodcuts. Post 8vo, 10s. 6d.; or Large Paper, 8vo, 15s.

————— History of Painting in North Italy, from 14th to 16th Century. Derived from Researches into the Works of Art in that Country. With Illustrations. 2 Vols. 8vo. 42s.

CUNYNGHAME'S (SIR ARTHUR) Travels in the Eastern Caucasus, on the Caspian, and Black Seas, in Daghestan and the Frontiers of Persia and Turkey. With Map and Illustrations. 8vo. 18s.

CURTIUS' (PROFESSOR) Student's Greek Grammar, for the Upper Forms. Edited by DR. WM. SMITH. Post 8vo. 6s.

————— Elucidations of the above Grammar. Translated by EVELYN ABBOT. Post 8vo. 7s. 6d.

————— Smaller Greek Grammar for the Middle and Lower Forms. Abridged from the larger work. 12mo. 3s. 6d.

————— Accidence of the Greek Language. Extracted from the above work. 12mo. 2s. 6d.

————— Principles of Greek Etymology. Translated by A. S. WILKINS, M.A., and E. B. ENGLAND, B.A. Vol. I. 8vo. 15s.

CURZON'S (HON. ROBERT) ARMENIA AND ERZEROUM. A Year on the Frontiers of Russia, Turkey, and Persia. Woodcuts. Post 8vo. 7s. 6d.

————— Visits to the Monasteries of the Levant. Illustrations. Post 8vo. 7s. 6d.

CUST'S (GENERAL) Warriors of the 17th Century—The Thirty Years' War. 2 Vols. 16s. Civil Wars of France and England. 2 Vols. 16s. Commanders of Fleets and Armies. 2 Vols. 18s.

————— Annals of the Wars—18th & 19th Century, 1700—1815. With Maps. 9 Vols. Post 8vo. 5s. each.

DAVIS'S (NATHAN) Ruined Cities of Numidia and Carthaginia. Illustrations. 8vo. 16s.

DAVY'S (SIR HUMPHRY) Consolations in Travel; or, Last Days of a Philosopher. Woodcuts. Fcap. 8vo. 3s. 6d.

————— Salmonia; or, Days of Fly Fishing. Woodcuts. Fcap. 8vo. 3s. 6d.

DARWIN'S (CHARLES) Journal of a Naturalist during a Voyage round the World. Crown 8vo. 9s.

————— Origin of Species by Means of Natural Selection; or, the Preservation of Favoured Races in the Struggle for Life. Crown 8vo. 7s. 6d.

————— Variation of Animals and Plants under Domestication. With Illustrations. 2 Vols. Crown 8vo. 18s.

————— Descent of Man, and Selection in Relation to Sex. With Illustrations. Crown 8vo. 9s.

————— Expressions of the Emotions in Man and Animals. With Illustrations. Crown 8vo. 12s.

————— Fertilization of Orchids through Insect Agency, and as to the good of Intercrossing. Woodcuts. Post 8vo. 9s.

————— Movements and Habits of Climbing Plants. Woodcuts. Crown 8vo. 6s.

————— Insectivorous Plants. Woodcuts. Crown 8vo. 14s.

————— Fact and Argument for Darwin. By FRITZ MULLER. Translated by W. S. DALLAS. Woodcuts. Post 8vo. 6s.

DELEPIERRE'S (Octave) History of Flemish Literature. 8vo. 9s.

———— Historic Difficulties & Contested Events. Post 8vo. 6s.

DENISON'S (E. B.) Life of Bishop Lonsdale. With Selections from his Writings. With Portrait. Crown 8vo. 10s. 6d.

DERBY'S (Earl of) Iliad of Homer rendered into English Blank Verse. 2 Vols. Post 8vo. 10s.

DE ROS'S (Lord) Young Officer's Companion; or, Essays on Military Duties and Qualities. with Examples and Illustrations from History. Post 8vo. 9s.

DEUTSCH'S (Emanuel) Talmud, Islam, The Targums and other Literary Remains. 8vo. 12s.

DILKE'S (Sir C. W.) Papers of a Critic. Selected from the Writings of the late Chas. Wentworth Dilke. With a Biographical Sketch. 2 Vols. 8vo. 24s.

DOG-BREAKING ; the Most Expeditious, Certain, and Easy Method, whether great excellence or only mediocrity he required. With a Few Hints for those who Love the Dog and the Gun. By Lieut.-Gen. Hutchinson. With 40 Woodcuts. Crown 8vo. 9s.

DOMESTIC MODERN COOKERY. Founded on Principles of Economy and Practical Knowledge, and adapted for Private Families. Woodcuts. Fcap. 8vo. 5s.

DOUGLAS'S (Sir Howard) Life and Adventures. Portrait. 8vo. 15s.

———— Theory and Practice of Gunnery. Plates. 8vo. 21s.

———— Construction of Bridges and the Passage of Rivers, in Military Operations. Plates. 8vo. 21s.

———— (Wm.) Horse-Shoeing; As it Is, and As it Should be. Illustrations. Post 8vo. 7s. 6d.

DRAKE'S (Sir Francis) Life, Voyages, and Exploits, by Sea and Land. By John Barrow. Post 8vo. 2s.

DRINKWATER'S (John) History of the Siege of Gibraltar, 1779-1783. With a Description and Account of that Garrison from the Earliest Periods. Post 8vo. 2s.

DUCANGE'S Mediæval Latin-English Dictionary. Translated by Rev. E. A. Dayman, M.A. Small 4to. [In preparation.

DU CHAILLU'S (Paul B.) Equatorial Africa, with Accounts of the Gorilla, the Nest-building Ape, Chimpanzee, Crocodile, &c. Illustrations. 8vo. 21s.

———— Journey to Ashango Land; and Further Penetration into Equatorial Africa. Illustrations. 8vo. 21s.

DUFFERIN'S (Lord) Letters from High 'Latitudes; a Yacht Voyage to Iceland, Jan Mayen, and Spitzbergen. Woodcuts. Post 8vo. 7s. 6d.

DUNCAN'S (Major) History of the Royal Artillery. Compiled from the Original Records. With Portraits. 2 Vols. 8vo. 30s.

DYER'S (Thos. H.) History of Modern Europe, from the taking of Constantinople by the Turks to the close of the War in the Crimea. With Index. 4 Vols. 8vo. 42s.

EASTLAKE'S (Sir Charles) Contributions to the Literature of the Fine Arts. With Memoir of the Author, and Selections from his Correspondence. By Lady Eastlake. 2 Vols. 8vo. 24s.

EDWARDS' (W. H.) Voyage up the River Amazons, including a Visit to Para. Post 8vo. 2s.

EIGHT MONTHS AT ROME, during the Vatican Council, with a Daily Account of the Proceedings. By POMPONIO LETO. Translated from the Original. 8vo. [*Nearly ready.*

ELDON'S (LORD) Public and Private Life, with Selections from his Correspondence and Diaries. By HORACE TWISS. Portrait. 2 Vols. Post 8vo. 21s.

ELGIN'S (LORD) Letters and Journals. Edited by THEODORE WALROND. With Preface by Dean Stanley. 8vo. 14s.

ELLESMERE'S (LORD) Two Sieges of Vienna by the Turks. Translated from the German. Post 8vo. 2s.

ELLIS'S (W.) Madagascar, including a Journey to the Capital, with notices of Natural History and the People. Woodcuts. 8vo. 16s.

———————— Madagascar Revisited. Setting forth the Persecutions and Heroic Sufferings of the Native Christians. Illustrations. 8vo. 16s.

———————— Memoir. By His Son. With his Character and Work. By REV. HENRY ALLON, D.D. Portrait. 8vo. 10s. 6d.

———————— (ROBINSON) Poems and Fragments of Catullus. 16mo. 5s.

ELPHINSTONE'S (HON. MOUNTSTUART) History of India—the Hindoo and Mahomedan Periods. Edited by PROFESSOR COWELL. Map. 8vo. 18s.

——————————(H. W.) Patterns for Turning; Comprising Elliptical and other Figures cut on the Lathe without the use of any Ornamental Chuck. With 70 Illustrations. Small 4to. 15s.

ENGLAND. See CALLCOTT, CROKER, HUME, MARKHAM, SMITH, and STANHOPE.

ESSAYS ON CATHEDRALS. With an Introduction. By DEAN HOWSON. 8vo. 12s.

CONTENTS.

Recollections of a Dean.—Bishop of Carlisle.
Cathedral Canons and their Work.—Canon Norris
Cathedrals in Ireland, Past and Future.—Dean of Cashel.
Cathedrals in their Missionary Aspect.—A. J. B. Beresford Hope.
Cathedral Foundations in Relation to Religious Thought.—Canon Westcott.

Cathedral Churches of the Old Foundation.—Edward A. Freeman.
Welsh Cathedrals.—Canon Perowne.
Education of Choristers.—Sir F. Gore Ouseley.
Cathedral Schools.—Canon Durham.
Cathedral Reform.—Chancellor Massingberd.
Relation of the Chapter to the Bishop. Chancellor Benson.
Architecture of the Cathedral Churches.—Canon Venables.

ELZE'S (KARL) Life of Lord Byron. With a Critical Essay on his Place in Literature. Translated from the German. With Portrait. 8vo. 16s.

FARRAR'S (A. S.) Critical History of Free Thought in reference to the Christian Religion. 8vo. 16s.

FERGUSSON'S (JAMES) History of Architecture in all Countries from the Earliest Times. With 1,600 Illustrations. 4 Vols. Medium 8vo. 31s. 6d. each.

Vol. I. & II. Ancient and Mediæval. Vol. III. Indian and Eastern. Vol. IV. Modern.

———————— Rude Stone Monuments in all Countries; their Age and Uses. With 230 Illustrations. Medium 8vo. 24s.

———————— Holy Sepulchre and the Temple at Jerusalem. Woodcuts. 8vo. 7s. 6d.

FLEMING'S (Professor) Student's Manual of Moral Philosophy. With Quotations and References. Post 8vo. 7s. 6d.

FLOWER GARDEN. By Rev. Thos. James. Fcap. 8vo. 1s.

FORD'S (Richard) Gatherings from Spain. Post 8vo. 3s. 6d.

FORSYTH'S (William) Life and Times of Cicero. With Selections from his Correspondence and Orations. Illustrations. 8vo. 10s. 6d.

———— Hortensius; an Historical Essay on the Office and Duties of an Advocate. Illustrations. 8vo. 12s.

———— History of Ancient Manuscripts. Post 8vo. 2s. 6d.

———— Novels and Novelists of the 18th Century, in Illustration of the Manners and Morals of the Age. Post 8vo. 10s. 6d.

FORTUNE'S (Robert) Narrative of Two Visits to the Tea Countries of China, 1843-52. Woodcuts. 2 Vols. Post 8vo. 18s.

FORSTER'S (John) Life of Jonathan Swift. Vol. I. 1667-1711. With Portrait. 8vo. 15s.

FOSS' (Edward) Biographia Juridica, or Biographical Dictionary of the Judges of England, from the Conquest to the Present Time, 1066-1870. Medium 8vo. 21s.

———— Tabulæ Curiales; or, Tables of the Superior Courts of Westminster Hall. Showing the Judges who sat in them from 1066 to 1864. 8vo. 10s. 6d.

FRANCE. *₊* See Markham—Smith—Student's.

FRENCH (The) in Algiers; The Soldier of the Foreign Legion— and the Prisoners of Abd-el-Kadir. Translated by Lady Duff Gordon. Post 8vo. 2s.

FRERE'S (Sir Bartle) Indian Missions. Small 8vo. 2s. 6d.

— —— Eastern Africa as a field for Missionary Labour. With Map. Crown 8vo. 5s.

——— Bengal Famine. How it will be Met and How to Prevent Future Famines in India. With Maps. Crown 8vo. 5s.

GALTON'S (Francis) Art of Travel; or, Hints on the Shifts and Contrivances available in Wild Countries. Woodcuts. Post 8vo. 7s. 6d.

GEOGRAPHICAL SOCIETY'S JOURNAL. (*Published Yearly.*)

GEORGE'S (Ernest) Mosel; a Series of Twenty Etchings, with Descriptive Letterpress. Imperial 4to. 42s.

——— Loire and South of France; a Series of Twenty Etchings, with Descriptive Text. Folio. 42s.

GERMANY (History of). See Markham.

GIBBON'S (Edward) History of the Decline and Fall of the Roman Empire. Edited by Milman and Guizot. Edited, with Notes, by Dr. Wm. Smith. Maps. 8 Vols. 8vo. 60s.

——— (The Student's Gibbon); Being an Epitome of the above work, incorporating the Researches of Recent Commentators. By Dr. Wm. Smith. Woodcuts. Post 8vo. 7s. 6d.

GIFFARD'S (EDWARD) Deeds of Naval Daring; or, Anecdotes of the British Navy. Fcap. 8vo. 3s. 6d.

GLADSTONE'S (W. E.) Financial Statements of 1853, 1860, 63–65. 8vo. 12s.

———— Rome and the Newest Fashions in Religion. Three Tracts. *Collected Edition.* With a new Preface. 8vo. 7s. 6d.

GLEIG'S (G. R.) Campaigns of the British Army at Washington and New Orleans. Post 8vo. 2s.

———— Story of the Battle of Waterloo. Post 8vo. 3s. 6d.

———— Narrative of Sale's Brigade in Affghanistan. Post 8vo. 2s.

———— Life of Lord Clive. Post 8vo. 3s. 6d.

———————— Sir Thomas Munro. Post 8vo. 3s. 6d.

GOLDSMITH'S (OLIVER) Works. Edited with Notes by PETER CUNNINGHAM. Vignettes. 4 Vols. 8vo. 30s.

GORDON'S (SIR ALEX.) Sketches of German Life, and Scenes from the War of Liberation. Post 8vo. 3s. 6d.

———————— (LADY DUFF) Amber-Witch: A Trial for Witchcraft. Post 8vo. 2s.

———————— French in Algiers. 1. The Soldier of the Foreign Legion. 2. The Prisoners of Abd-el-Kadir. Post 8vo. 2s.

GRAMMARS. See CURTIUS; HALL; HUTTON; KING EDWARD; MATTHIÆ; MAETZNER; SMITH.

GREECE. *See* GROTE—SMITH—Student.

GREY'S (EARL) Correspondence with King William IVth and Sir Herbert Taylor, from 1830 to 1832. 2 Vols. 8vo. 30s.

———————— Parliamentary Government and Reform; with Suggestions for the Improvement of our Representative System. *Second Edition.* 8vo.

GUIZOT'S (M.) Meditations on Christianity, and on the Religious Questions of the Day. 3 Vols. Post 8vo.

GROTE'S (GEORGE) History of Greece. From the Earliest Times to the close of the generation contemporary with the death of Alexander the Great. *Library Edition.* Portrait, Maps, and Plans. 10 Vols. 8vo. 120s. *Cabinet Edition.* Portrait and Plans. 12 Vols. Post 8vo. 6s. each.

———————— PLATO, and other Companions of Socrates. 3 Vols. 8vo. 45s.

———————— ARISTOTLE. 2 Vols. 8vo. 32s.

———————— Minor Works. With Critical Remarks on his Intellectual Character, Writings, and Speeches. By ALEX. BAIN, LL.D. Portrait. 8vo. 14s.

———————— Fragments on Ethical Subjects. Being a Selection from his Posthumous Papers. With an Introduction. By ALEXANDER BAIN, M.A. 8vo.

———————— Personal Life. Compiled from Family Documents, Private Memoranda, and Original Letters to and from Various Friends. By Mrs. Grote. Portrait. 8vo. 12s.

———————— (MRS.) Memoir of Ary Scheffer. Portrait. 8vo. 8s. 6d.

HALL'S (T. D.) School Manual of English Grammar. With Copious Exercises. 12mo. 3s. 6d.

———————— Primary English Grammar for Elementary Schools. 16mo. 1s.

———————— Child's First Latin Book, including a Systematic Treatment of the New Pronunciation, and a full Praxis of Nouns, Adjectives, and Pronouns. 16mo. 1s. 6d.

HALLAM'S (HENRY) Constitutional History of England, from the
Accession of Henry the Seventh to the Death of George the Second.
Library Edition. 3 Vols. 8vo. 30s. *Cabinet Edition,* 3 Vols. Post 8vo. 12s.

———— Student's Edition of the above work. Edited by
WM. SMITH, D.C.L. Post 8vo. 7s. 6d.

———— History of Europe during the Middle Ages. *Library
Edition.* 3 Vols. 8vo. 30s. *Cabinet Edition,* 3 Vols. Post 8vo. 12s.

———— Student's Edition of the above work. Edited by
WM. SMITH, D.C.L. Post 8vo. 7s. 6d.

———— Literary History of Europe, during the 15th, 16th and
17th Centuries. *Library Edition.* 3 Vols. 8vo. 36s. *Cabinet Edition.*
4 Vols. Post 8vo. 16s.

———— (ARTHUR) Literary Remains; in Verse and Prose.
Portrait. Fcap. 8vo. 3s. 6d.

HAMILTON'S (GEN. SIR F. W.) History of the Grenadier Guards.
From Original Documents in the Rolls' Records, War Office, Regimental
Records, &c. With Illustrations. 3 Vols. 8vo. 63s.

HART'S ARMY LIST. (*Published Quarterly and Annually.*)

HAY'S (SIR J. H. DRUMMOND) Western Barbary, its Wild Tribes
and Savage Animals. Post 8vo. 2s.

HEAD'S (SIR FRANCIS) Royal Engineer. Illustrations. 8vo. 12s.

——— Life of Sir John Burgoyne. Post 8vo. 1s.

——— Rapid Journeys across the Pampas. Post 8vo. 2s.

——— Bubbles from the Brunnen of Nassau. Illustrations.
Post 8vo. 7s. 6d.

——— Emigrant. Fcap. 8vo. 2s. 6d.

——— Stokers and Pokers; or, the London and North Western
Railway. Post 8vo. 2s.

——— (SIR EDMUND) Shall and Will; or, Future Auxiliary
Verbs. Fcap. 8vo. 4s.

HEBER'S (BISHOP) Journals in India. 2 Vols. Post 8vo. 7s.

——— Poetical Works. Portrait. Fcap. 8vo. 3s. 6d.

——— Hymns adapted to the Church Service. 16mo. 1s. 6d.

HERODOTUS. A New English Version. Edited, with Notes
and Essays, historical, ethnographical, and geographical, by CANON
RAWLINSON, assisted by SIR HENRY RAWLINSON and SIR J. G. WIL-
KINSON. Maps and Woodcuts. 4 Vols. 8vo. 48s.

HERSCHEL'S (CAROLINE) Memoir and Correspondence. By
MRS. JOHN HERSCHEL. With Portraits. Crown 8vo.

HATHERLEY'S (LORD) Continuity of Scripture, as Declared
by the Testimony of our Lord and of the Evangelists and Apostles.
8vo. 6s. *Popular Edition.* Post 8vo. 2s. 6d.

HOLLWAY'S (J. G.) Month in Norway. Fcap. 8vo. 2s.

HONEY BEE. By REV. THOMAS JAMES. Fcap. 8vo. 1s.

HOOK'S (DEAN) Church Dictionary. 8vo. 16s.

——— (THEODORE) Life. By J. G. LOCKHART. Fcap. 8vo. 1s.

HOPE'S (T. C.) ARCHITECTURE OF AHMEDABAD, with Historical
Sketch and Architectural Notes. With Maps, Photographs, and
Woodcuts. 4to. 5l. 5s.

——— (A. J. BERESFORD) Worship in the Church of England.
8vo. 9s., or, *Popular Selections from.* 8vo. 2s. 6d.

FOREIGN HANDBOOKS.

HAND-BOOK—TRAVEL-TALK. English, French, German, and
Italian. 18mo. 3s. 6d.

———— -- HOLLAND,—Belgium, Rhenish Prussia, and the
Rhine from Holland to Mayence. Map and Plans. Post 8vo. 6s.

———— NORTH GERMANY,—From the Baltic to the
Black Forest, the Hartz, Thüringerwald, Saxon Switzerland, Rügen,
the Giant Mountains, Taunus, Odenwald, and the Rhine Countries,
from Frankfort to Basle. Map and Plans. Post 8vo. 6s.

———— SOUTH GERMANY, — Wurtemburg, Bavaria,
Austria, Styria, Salzburg, the Austrian and Bavarian Alps, Tyrol, Hungary, and the Danube, from Ulm to the Black Sea. Map. Post 8vo. 10s.

———— PAINTING. German, Flemish, and Dutch Schools.
Illustrations. 2 Vols. Post 8vo. 24s.

———— LIVES OF EARLY FLEMISH PAINTERS. By
Crowe and Cavalcaselle. Illustrations. Post 8vo. 10s. 6d.

———— SWITZERLAND, Alps of Savoy, and Piedmont.
Maps. Post 8vo. 9s.

———— FRANCE, Part I. Normandy, Brittany, the French
Alps, the Loire, the Seine, the Garonne, and the Pyrenees. Post 8vo.
7s. 6d.

———— - Part II. Central France, Auvergne, the
Cevennes, Burgundy, the Rhone and Saone, Provence, Nimes, Arles,
Marseilles, the French Alps, Alsace, Lorraine, Champagne, &c. Maps.
Post 8vo. 7s. 6d.

———— MEDITERRANEAN ISLANDS—Malta, Corsica,
Sardinia, and Sicily. Maps. Post 8vo. [In the Press.

———— ALGERIA. Algiers, Constantine, Oran, the Atlas
Range. Map. Post 8vo. 9s.

———— PARIS, and its Environs. Map. 16mo. 3s. 6d.
⁎ Murray's Plan of Paris, mounted on canvas. 3s. 6d.

———— SPAIN, Madrid, The Castiles, The Basque Provinces,
Leon, The Asturias, Galicia, Estremadura, Andalusia, Ronda, Granada,
Murcia, Valencia, Catalonia, Aragon, Navarre, The Balearic Islands,
&c. &c. Maps. 2 Vols. Post 8vo. 24s.

———— PORTUGAL, Lisbon, Porto, Cintra, Mafra, &c.
Map. Post 8vo. 9s.

———— NORTH ITALY, Turin, Milan, Cremona, the
Italian Lakes, Bergamo, Brescia, Verona, Mantua, Vicenza, Padua,
Ferrara, Bologna, Ravenna, Rimini, Piacenza, Genoa, the Riviera,
Venice, Parma, Modena, and Romagna. Map. Post 8vo. 10s.

———— CENTRAL ITALY, Florence, Lucca, Tuscany, The
Marches, Umbria, and the late Patrimony of St. Peter's. Map. Post 8vo.
10s.

———— ROME and its Environs. Map. Post 8vo. 10s.

———— SOUTH ITALY, Two Sicilies, Naples, Pompeii,
Herculaneum, and Vesuvius. Map. Post 8vo. 10s.

———— KNAPSACK GUIDE TO ITALY. 16mo.

———— PAINTING. The Italian Schools. Illustrations.
2 Vols. Post 8vo. 30s.

———— LIVES OF ITALIAN PAINTERS, from Cimabue
to Bassano. By Mrs. Jameson. Portraits. Post 8vo. 12s.

———— NORWAY, Christiania, Bergen, Trondhjem. The
Fjelds and Fjords. Map. Post 8vo. 9s.

———— SWEDEN, Stockholm, Upsala, Gothenburg, the
Shores of the Baltic, &c. Post 8vo. 6s.

———— DENMARK, Sleswig, Holstein, Copenhagen, Jutland,
Iceland. Map. Post 8vo. 6s.

HAND-BOOK--RUSSIA, St. Petersburg, Moscow, Poland, and Finland. Maps. Post 8vo. 15s.

———— GREECE, the Ionian Islands, Continental Greece, Athens, the Peloponnesus, the Islands of the Ægean Sea, Albania, Thessaly, and Macedonia. Maps. Post 8vo. 15s.

———— TURKEY IN ASIA—Constantinople, the Bosphorus, Dardanelles, Brousa, Plain of Troy, Crete, Cyprus, Smyrna, Ephesus, the Seven Churches, Coasts of the Black Sea, Armenia, Mesopotamia, &c. Maps. Post 8vo. 15s.

———— EGYPT, including Descriptions of the Course of the Nile through Egypt and Nubia, Alexandria, Cairo, and Thebes, the Suez Canal, the Pyramids, the Peninsula of Sinai, the Oases, the Fyoom, &c. Map. Post 8vo. 15s

———— HOLY LAND—Syria, Palestine, Peninsula of Sinai, Edom, Syrian Deserts, Petra, Damascus, and Palmyra. Maps. Post 8vo.

   *** Travelling Map of Palestine. In a case. 12s.

———— INDIA — Bombay and Madras. Map. 2 Vols. Post 8vo. 12s. each.

ENGLISH HANDBOOKS.

HAND-BOOK—MODERN LONDON. Map. 16mo. 3s. 6d.

———— EASTERN COUNTIES, Chelmsford, Harwich, Colchester, Maldon, Cambridge, Ely, Newmarket, Bury St. Edmunds, Ipswich, Woodbridge, Felixstowe, Lowestoft, Norwich, Yarmouth, Cromer, &c. Map and Plans. Post 8vo. 12s.

———— CATHEDRALS of Oxford, Peterborough, Norwich, Ely, and Lincoln. With 90 Illustrations. Crown 8vo. 18s.

———— KENT AND SUSSEX, Canterbury, Dover, Ramsgate, Sheerness, Rochester, Chatham, Woolwich, Brighton, Chichester, Worthing, Hastings, Lewes, Arundel, &c. Map. Post 8vo. 10s.

———— SURREY AND HANTS, Kingston, Croydon, Reigate, Guildford, Dorking, Boxhill, Winchester, Southampton, New Forest, Portsmouth, and Isle of Wight. Maps. Post 8vo. 10s.

———— BERKS, BUCKS, AND OXON, Windsor, Eton, Reading, Aylesbury, Uxbridge, Wycombe, Henley, the City and University of Oxford, Blenheim, and the Descent of the Thames. Map. Post 8vo. 7s. 6d.

———— WILTS, DORSET, AND SOMERSET, Salisbury, Chippenham, Weymouth, Sherborne, Wells, Bath, Bristol, Taunton, &c. Map. Post 8vo. 10s.

———— DEVON AND CORNWALL, Exeter, Ilfracombe, Linton, Sidmouth, Dawlish, Teignmouth, Plymouth, Devonport, Torquay, Launceston, Truro, Penzance, Falmouth, the Lizard, Land's End, &c. Maps. Post 8vo. 12s.

————CATHEDRALS of Winchester, Salisbury, Exeter, Wells, Chichester, Rochester, Canterbury. With 110 Illustrations. 2 Vols. Crown 8vo. 24s.

———— GLOUCESTER, HEREFORD, and WORCESTER, Cirencester, Cheltenham, Stroud, Tewkesbury, Leominster, Ross, Malvern, Kidderminster, Dudley, Bromsgrove, Evesham. Map. Post 8vo. 9s.

———— CATHEDRALS of Bristol, Gloucester, Hereford, Worcester, and Lichfield. With 50 Illustrations. Crown 8vo. 16s.

———— NORTH WALES, Bangor, Carnarvon, Beaumaris, Snowdon, Llanberis, Dolgelly, Cader Idris, Conway, &c. Map. Post 8vo. 7s.

———— SOUTH WALES, Monmouth, Llandaff, Merthyr, Vale of Neath, Pembroke, Carmarthen, Tenby, Swansea, and The Wye, &c. Map. Post 8vo. 7s.

HAND-BOOK—CATHEDRALS OF BANGOR, ST. ASAPH,
Llandaff, and St. David's. With Illustrations. Post 8vo. 15s.

———— **DERBY, NOTTS, LEICESTER, STAFFORD,**
Matlock, Bakewell, Chatsworth, The Peak, Buxton, Hardwick, Dove
Dale, Ashborne, Southwell, Mansfield, Retford, Burton, Belvoir, Melton
Mowbray, Wolverhampton, Lichfield, Walsall, Tamworth. Map.
Post 8vo. 9s.

———— **SHROPSHIRE, CHESHIRE AND LANCASHIRE**
—Shrewsbury, Ludlow, Bridgnorth, Oswestry, Chester, Crewe, Alderley,
Stockport, Birkenhead, Warrington, Bury, Manchester, Liverpool,
Burnley, Clitheroe, Bolton, Blackburn, Wigan, Preston, Rochdale,
Lancaster, Southport, Blackpool, &c. Map. Post 8vo. 10s.

———— **YORKSHIRE, Doncaster, Hull, Selby, Beverley,**
Scarborough, Whitby, Harrogate, Ripon, Leeds, Wakefield, Bradford,
Halifax, Huddersfield, Sheffield. Map and Plans. Post 8vo. 12s.

———— **CATHEDRALS of York, Ripon, Durham, Carlisle,**
Chester, and Manchester. With 60 Illustrations. 2 Vols. Crown 8vo.
21s.

———— **DURHAM AND NORTHUMBERLAND, New-**
castle, Darlington, Gateshead, Bishop Auckland, Stockton, Hartlepool,
Sunderland, Shields, Berwick-on-Tweed, Morpeth, Tynemouth, Cold-
stream, Alnwick, &c. Map. Post 8vo. 9s.

———— **WESTMORLAND AND CUMBERLAND—Lan-**
caster, Furness Abbey, Ambleside, Kendal, Windermere, Coniston,
Keswick, Grasmere, Ulswater, Carlisle, Cockermouth, Penrith, Appleby,
Map. Post 8vo. 6s.

*** MURRAY'S MAP OF THE LAKE DISTRICT, on canvas. 3s. 6d.

———— **SCOTLAND, Edinburgh, Melrose, Kelso, Glasgow,**
Dumfries, Ayr, Stirling, Arran, The Clyde, Oban, Inverary, Loch
Lomond, Loch Katrine and Trossachs, Caledonian Canal, Inverness,
Perth, Dundee, Aberdeen, Braemar, Skye, Caithness, Ross, Suther-
land, &c. Maps and Plans. Post 8vo. 9s.

———— **IRELAND, Dublin, Belfast, Donegal, Galway,**
Wexford, Cork, Limerick, Waterford, Killarney, Munster, &c. Maps.
Post 8vo. 12s.

HORACE; a New Edition of the Text. Edited by DEAN MILMAN.
With 100 Woodcuts. Crown 8vo. 7s. 6d.

———— Life of. By DEAN MILMAN. Illustrations. 8vo. 9s.

HOUGHTON'S (LORD) Monographs, Vol. I., Personal and Social.
With Portraits. Crown 8vo. 10s. 6d.

———— POETICAL WORKS. *Collected Edition.* With Portrait 2 Vols Fcap. 8vo. 12s.

HUME'S (The Student's) History of England, from the Inva-
sion of Julius Cæsar to the Revolution of 1688. Corrected and continued to 1868. Woodcuts. Post 8vo. 7s. 6d.

HUTCHINSON (GEN.), on the most expeditious, certain, and
easy Method of Dog-Breaking. With 40 Illustrations. Crown 8vo.
9s.

HUTTON'S (H. E.) Principia Græca; an Introduction to the Study
of Greek. Comprehending Grammar, Delectus, and Exercise-book,
with Vocabularies. *Sixth Edition.* 12mo. 3s. 6d.

IRBY AND MANGLES' Travels in Egypt, Nubia, Syria, and
the Holy Land. Post 8vo. 2s.

JACOBSON'S (BISH P) Fragmentary Illustrations of the History
of the Book of Common Prayer; from Manuscript Sources (Bishop
SANDERSON and Bishop WREN). 8vo. 5s.

JAMES' (REV. THOMAS) Fables of Æsop. A New Translation, with
Historical Preface. With 100 Woodcuts by TENNIEL and WOLF.
Post 8vo. 2s. 6d.

c

HOME AND COLONIAL LIBRARY. A Series of Works adapted for all circles and classes of Readers, having been selected for their acknowledged interest, and ability of the Authors. Post 8vo. Published at 2s. and 3s. 6d. each, and arranged under two distinctive heads as follows :—

CLASS A.

HISTORY, BIOGRAPHY, AND HISTORIC TALES.

1. SIEGE OF GIBRALTAR. By John Drinkwater. 2s.

2. THE AMBER-WITCH. By Lady Duff Gordon. 2s.

3. CROMWELL AND BUNYAN. By Robert Southey. 2s.

4. LIFE of Sir FRANCIS DRAKE. By John Barrow. 2s.

5. CAMPAIGNS AT WASHINGTON. By Rev. G. R. Gleig. 2s.

6. THE FRENCH IN ALGIERS. By Lady Duff Gordon. 2s.

7. THE FALL OF THE JESUITS. 2s.

8. LIVONIAN TALES. 2s.

9. LIFE OF CONDÉ. By Lord Mahon. 3s. 6d.

10. SALE'S BRIGADE. By Rev. G. R. Gleig. 2s.

11. THE SIEGES OF VIENNA. By Lord Ellesmere. 2s.

12. THE WAYSIDE CROSS. By Capt. Milman. 2s.

13. SKETCHES of GERMAN LIFE. By Sir A. Gordon. 3s. 6d.

14. THE BATTLE of WATERLOO. By Rev. G. R. Gleig. 3s. 6d.

15. AUTOBIOGRAPHY OF STEFFENS. 2s.

16. THE BRITISH POETS. By Thomas Campbell. 3s. 6d.

17. HISTORICAL ESSAYS. By Lord Mahon. 3s. 6d.

18. LIFE OF LORD CLIVE. By Rev. G. R. Gleig. 3s. 6d.

19. NORTH - WESTERN RAILWAY. By Sir F. B. Head. 2s.

20. LIFE OF MUNRO. By Rev. G. R. Gleig. 3s. 6d.

CLASS B.

VOYAGES, TRAVELS, AND ADVENTURES.

1. BIBLE IN SPAIN. By George Borrow. 3s. 6d.

2. GYPSIES of SPAIN. By George Borrow. 3s. 6d.

3 & 4. JOURNALS IN INDIA. By Bishop Heber. 2 Vols. 7s.

5. TRAVELS in the HOLY LAND. By Irby and Mangles. 2s.

6. MOROCCO AND THE MOORS. By J. Drummond Hay. 2s.

7. LETTERS FROM the BALTIC. By a Lady. 2s.

8. NEW SOUTH WALES. By Mrs. Meredith. 2s.

9. THE WEST INDIES. By M. G. Lewis. 2s.

10. SKETCHES OF PERSIA. By Sir John Malcolm. 3s. 6d.

11. MEMOIRS OF FATHER RIPA. 2s.

12 & 13. TYPEE AND OMOO. By Hermann Melville. 2 Vols. 7s.

14. MISSIONARY LIFE IN CANADA. By Rev. J. Abbott. 2s.

15. LETTERS FROM MADRAS. By a Lady. 2s.

16. HIGHLAND SPORTS. By Charles St. John. 3s. 6d.

17. PAMPAS JOURNEYS. By Sir F. B. Head. 2s.

18. GATHERINGS FROM SPAIN. By Richard Ford. 3s. 6d.

19. THE RIVER AMAZON. By W. H. Edwards. 2s.

20. MANNERS & CUSTOMS OF INDIA. By Rev. C. Acland 2s.

21. ADVENTURES IN MEXICO. By G. F. Ruxton. 3s. 6d.

22. PORTUGAL AND GALLICIA. By Lord Carnarvon. 3s. 6d.

23. BUSH LIFE IN AUSTRALIA. By Rev. H. W. Haygarth. 2s.

24. THE LIBYAN DESERT. By Bayle St. John. 2s.

25. SIERRA LEONE. By A Lady. 3s. 6d.

. Each work may be had separately.

JAMESON'S (MRS.) Lives of the Early Italian Painters—
and the Progress of Painting in Italy—Cimabue to Bassano. With
50 Portraits' Post 8vo. 12s.

JENNINGS' (L. J.) Eighty Years of Republican Government in
the United States. Post 8vo. 10s. 6d.

JERVIS'S (REV. W. H.) Gallican Church, from the Con-
cordat of Bologna, 1516, to the Revolution. With an Introduction.
Portraits. 2 Vols. 8vo. 28s.

JESSE'S (EDWARD) Gleanings in Natural History. Fcp 8vo. 3s. 6d.

JEX-BLAKE'S (REV. T. W.) Life in Faith : Sermons Preached
at Cheltenham and Rugby. Fcap. 8vo.

JOHNS' (REV. B. G.) Blind People ; their Works and Ways. With
Sketches of the Lives of some famous Blind Men. With Illustrations.
Post 8vo. 7s. 6d.

JOHNSON'S (DR. SAMUEL) Life. By James Boswell. Including
the Tour to the Hebrides. Edited by MR. CROKER. New Edition.
Portraits. 4 Vols. 8vo. [In Preparation.

———— Lives of the most eminent English Poets, with
Critical Observations on their Works. Edited with Notes, Corrective
and Explanatory, by PETER CUNNINGHAM. 3 vols. 8vo. 22s. 6d.

JUNIUS' HANDWRITING Professionally investigated. By Mr. CHABOT,
Expert. With Preface and Collateral Evidence, by the Hon. EDWARD
TWISLETON. With Fac-similes, Woodcuts, &c. 4to. 4 3 3s.

KEN'S (BISHOP) Life. By a LAYMAN. Portrait. 2 Vols. 8vo. 18s.

———— Exposition of the Apostles' Creed. 16mo. 1s. 6d.

KERR'S (ROBERT) GENTLEMAN'S HOUSE ; OR, HOW TO PLAN ENG-
LISH RESIDENCES FROM THE PARSONAGE TO THE PALACE. With
Views and Plans. 8vo. 24s.

———— Small Country House. A Brief Practical Discourse on
the Planning of a Residence from 20 0l. to 5000l. With Supplementary Estimates to 7000l. Post 8vo. 3s.

———— Ancient Lights ; a Book for Architects, Surveyors,
Lawyers, and Landlords. 8vo. 5s. 6d.

———— (R. MALCOLM) Student's Blackstone. A Systematic
Abridgment of the entire Commentaries, adapted to the present state
of the law. Post 8vo. 7s. 6d.

KING EDWARD VIth's Latin Grammar. 12mo. 3s. 6d.

———— First Latin Book. 12mo. 2s 6d.

KING GEORGE IIIRD's Correspondence with Lord North,
1769-82. Edited, with Notes and Introduction, by W. BODHAM DONNE.
2 vols. 8vo. 32s.

KING'S (R. J.) Archæology, Travel and Art ; being Sketches and
Studies, Historical and Descriptive. 8vo. 12s.

KIRK'S (J. FOSTER) History of Charles the Bold, Duke of Burgundy. Portrait. 3 Vols. 8vo. 45s.

KIRKES' Handbook of Physiology. Edited by W. MORRANT
BAKER, F.R.C.S. With 240 Illustrations. Post 8vo. 12s. 6d.

KUGLER'S Handbook of Painting.—The Italian Schools. Revised and Remodelled from the most recent Researches. By LADY
EASTLAKE. With 140 Illustrations. 2 Vols. Crown 8vo. 30s.

———— Handbook of Painting.—The German, Flemish, and
Dutch Schools. Revised and in part re-written. By J. A. CROWE.
With 60 Illustrations. 2 Vols. Crown 8vo. 21s.

LANE'S (E. W.) Account of the Manners and Customs of Modern
Egyptians. With Illustrations. 2 Vols. Post 8vo. 12s

LAWRENCE'S (SIR GEO.) Reminiscences of Forty-three Years' Service in India; including Captivities in Cabul among the Affghans and among the Sikhs, and a Narrative of the Mutiny in Rajputana. Crown 8vo. 10s. 6d.

LAYARD'S (A. H.) Nineveh and its Remains. Being a Narrative of Researches and Discoveries amidst the Ruins of Assyria. With an Account of the Chaldean Christians of Kurdistan; the Yezedis, or Devil-worshippers; and an Enquiry into the Manners and Arts of the Ancient Assyrians. Plates and Woodcuts. 2 Vols. 8vo. 36s.
. A POPULAR EDITION of the above work. With Illustrations. Post 8vo. 7s. 6d.

———— Nineveh and Babylon; being the Narrative of Discoveries in the Ruins, with Travels in Armenia, Kurdistan and the Desert, during a Second Expedition to Assyria. With Map and Plates. 8vo. 21s.
. A POPULAR EDITION of the above work. With Illustrations. Post 8vo. 7s. 6d.

LEATHES' (STANLEY) Practical Hebrew Grammar. With the Hebrew Text of Genesis i.—vi., and Psalms i.—vi. Grammatical Analysis and Vocabulary. Post 8vo. 7s. 6d.

LENNEP'S (REV. H. J. VAN) Missionary Travels in Asia Minor. With Illustrations of Biblical History and Archæology. With Map and Woodcuts. 2 Vols. Post 8vo. 24s.

———— Modern Customs and Manners of Bible Lands in Illustration of Scripture. With Coloured Maps and 300 Illustrations. 2 Vols. 8vo. 21s.

LESLIE'S (C. R.) Handbook for Young Painters. With Illustrations. Post 8vo. 7s. 6d.

———— Life and Works of Sir Joshua Reynolds. Portraits and Illustrations. 2 Vols. 8vo. 42s.

LETTERS FROM THE BALTIC. By a LADY. Post 8vo. 2s.

———— MADRAS. By a LADY. Post 8vo. 2s.

———— SIERRA LEONE. By a LADY. Post 8vo. 3s. 6d.

LEVI'S (LEONE) History of British Commerce; and of the Economic Progress of the Nation, from 1763 to 1870. 8vo. 16s.

LIDDELL'S (DEAN) Student's History of Rome, from the earliest Times to the establishment of the Empire. With Woodcuts. Post 8vo. 7s. 6d.

LLOYD'S (W. WATKISS) History of Sicily to the Athenian War; with Elucidations of the Sicilian Odes of Pindar. With Map 8vo. 14s.

LISPINGS from LOW LATITUDES; or, the Journal of the Hon. Impulsia Gushington. Edited by LORD DUFFERIN. With 24 Plates. 4to 21s.

LITTLE ARTHUR'S HISTORY OF ENGLAND. By LADY CALLCOTT. New Edition, continued to 1872. With Woodcuts. Fcap. 8vo. 1s. 6d.

LIVINGSTONE'S (DR.) Popular Account of his First Expedition to Africa, 1840-56. Illustrations. Post 8vo. 7s. 6d.

———— Popular Account of his Second Expedition to Africa, 1858-64. Map and Illustrations. Post 8vo. 7s. 6d.

———— Last Journals in Central Africa, from 1865 to his Death. Continued by a Narrative of his last moments and sufferings. By Rev HORACE WALLER. Maps and Illustrations. 2 Vols 8vo. 28s.

LIVONIAN TALES. By the Author of "Letters from the Baltic." Post 8vo. 2s.

LOCH'S (H. B.) Personal Narrative of Events during Lord Elgin's Second Embassy to China. With Illustrations. Post 8vo. 9s.

LOCKHART'S (J. G.) Ancient Spanish Ballads. Historical and Romantic. Translated, with Notes. With Portrait and Illustrations. Crown 8vo. 5s.

———————— Life of Theodore Hook. Fcap. 8vo. 1s.

LONSDALE'S (Bishop) Life. With Selections from his Writings. By E. B. Denison. With Portrait. Crown 8vo. 10s. 6d.

LOUDON'S (Mrs.) Gardening for Ladies. With Directions and Calendar of Operations for Every Month. Woodcuts. Fcap. 8vo. 3s. 6d.

LUCKNOW: A Lady's Diary of the Siege. Fcap. 8vo. 4s. 6d.

LYELL'S (Sir Charles) Principles of Geology; or, the Modern Changes of the Earth and its Inhabitants considered as illustrative of Geology. With Illustrations. 2 Vols. 8vo. 32s.

———————— Student's Elements of Geology. With Table of British Fossils and 600 Illustrations. Post 8vo. 9s.

———————— Geological Evidences of the Antiquity of Man, including an Outline of Glacial Post-Tertiary Geology, and Remarks on the Origin of Species. Illustrations. 8vo. 14s.

———————— (K. M.) Geographical Handbook of Ferns. With Tables to show their Distribution. Post 8vo. 7s. 6d.

LYTTELTON'S (Lord) Ephemera. 2 Vols. Post 8vo. 19s. 6d.

LYTTON'S (Lord) Memoir of Julian Fane. With Portrait. Post 8vo. 5s

McCLINTOCK'S (Sir L.) Narrative of the Discovery of the Fate of Sir John Franklin and his Companions in the Arctic Seas. With Illustrations. Post 8vo. 7s. 6d.

MACDOUGALL'S (Col.) Modern Warfare as Influenced by Modern Artillery. With Plans. Post 8vo. 12s.

MACGREGOR'S (J.) Rob Roy on the Jordan, Nile, Red Sea, Gennesareth, &c. A Canoe Cruise in Palestine and Egypt and the Waters of Damascus. With Map and 70 Illustrations. Crown 8vo. 7s. 6d

MACPHERSON'S (Major) Services in India, while Political Agent at Gwalior during the Mutiny. Illustrations. 8vo. 12s.

MAETZNER'S English Grammar. A Methodical, Analytical, and Historical Treatise on the Orthography, Prosody, Inflections, and Syntax of the English Tongue. Translated from the German. By Clair J. Grece, LL.D. 3 Vols. 8vo. 36s.

MAHON (Lord), see Stanhope.

MAINE'S (Sir H. Sumner) Ancient Law: its Connection with the Early History of Society, and its Relation to Modern Ideas 8vo. 12s.

———————— Village Communities in the East and West. 8vo. 9s.

———————— Early History of Institutions. 8vo. 12s.

MALCOLM'S (Sir John) Sketches of Persia. Post 8vo. 3s. 6d.

MANSEL'S (Dean) Limits of Religious Thought Examined. Post 8vo. 8s. 6d.

———————— Letters. Lectures, and Papers, including the Phrontisterion, or Oxford in the XIXth Century. Edited by H. W. Chandler, M.A. 8vo. 12s.

———————— Gnostic Heresies of the First and Second Centuries. With a sketch of his life and character By Lord Carnarvon. Edited by Canon Lightfoot. 8vo 10s. 6d.

MANUAL OF SCIENTIFIC ENQUIRY. For the Use of Travellers. Edited by Rev. R. Main. Post 8vo. 3s. 6d. (Published by order of the Lords of the Admiralty.)

MARCO POLO. The Book of Ser Marco Polo, the Venetian. Concerning the Kingdoms and Marvels of the East. A new English Version. Illustrated by the light of Oriental Writers and Modern Travels. By Col. Henry Yule. Maps and Illustrations. 2 Vols. Medium 8vo. 63s.

MARKHAM'S (Mrs.) History of England. From the First Invasion by the Romans to 1867. Woodcuts. 12mo. 3s. 6d.

———————— **History of France. From the Conquest by the** Gauls to 1861. Woodcuts. 12mo, 3s. 6d.

———————— **History of Germany. From the Invasion by Marius** to 1867. Woodcuts. 12mo. 3s. 6d.

MARLBOROUGH'S (Sarah, Duchess of) Letters. Now first published from the Original MSS. at Madresfield Court. With an Introduction. 8vo. 10s. 6d.

MARRYAT'S (Joseph) History of Modern and Mediæval Pottery and Porcelain. With a Description of the Manufacture. Plates and Woodcuts. 8vo. 42s.

MARSH'S (G. P.) Student's Manual of the English Language. Post 8vo. 7s. 6d.

MATTHIÆ'S Greek Grammar. Abridged by Blomfield, Revised by E. S. Crooke. 12mo. 4s.

MAUREL'S Character, Actions, and Writings of Wellington. Fcap. 8vo. 1s. 6d.

MAYNE'S (Capt.) Four Years in British Columbia and Van- conver Island. Illustrations. 8vo. 16s.

MEADE'S (Hon. Herbert) Ride through the Disturbed Districts of New Zealand, with a Cruise among the South Sea Islands. With Illustrations. Medium 8vo. 12s.

MELVILLE'S (Hermann) Marquesas and South Sea Islands. 2 Vols. Post 8vo. 7s.

MEREDITH'S (Mrs. Charles) Notes and Sketches of New South Wales. Post 8vo. 2s.

MESSIAH (THE): The Life, Travels, Death, Resurrection, and Ascension of our Blessed Lord. By A Layman. Map. 8vo. 18s.

MILLINGTON'S (Rev. T. S.) Signs and Wonders in the Land of Ham, or the Ten Plagues of Egypt, with Ancient and Modern Illustrations. Woodcuts. Post 8vo. 7s. 6d.

MILMAN'S (Dean) History of the Jews, from the earliest Period down to Modern Times. 3 Vols. Post 8vo. 18s.

———————— **Early Christiani y, from the Birth of Christ to the** Abolition of Paganism in the Roman Empire. 3 Vols. Post 8vo. 18s.

———————— **Latin Christianity, including that of the Popes to** the Pontificate of Nicholas V. 9 Vols. Post 8vo. 54s.

———————— **Annals of St. Paul's Cathedral, from the Romans to** the funeral of Wellington. Portrait and Illustrations. 8vo. 18s.

———————— **Character and Conduct of the Apostles considered** as an Evidence of Christianity. 8vo. 10s. 6d.

———————— **Quinti Horatii Flacci Opera. With 100 Woodcuts.** Small 8vo. 7s. 6d.

———————— **Life of Quintus Horatius Flaccus. With Illustra-** tions. 8vo. 9s.

———————— **Poetical Works. The Fall of Jerusalem—Martyr of** Antioch—Balshazzar—Tamor—Anne Boleyn—Fazio, &c. With Portrait and Illustrations. 3 Vols. Fcap. 8vo. 18s.

Fall of Jerusalem. Fcap. 8vo. 1s.

———————— **(Capt. E. A.) Wayside Cross. Post 8vo. 2s.**

MIVART'S (St. George) Lessons from Nature; as manifested in Mind and Matter. 8vo.

MODERN DOMESTIC COOKERY. Founded on Principles of Economy and Practical Knowledge. New Edition. Woodcuts. Fcap. 8vo. 5s.

MONGREDIEN'S (Augustus) Trees and Shrubs for English Plantation. A Selection and Description of the most Ornamental which will flourish in the open air in our climate. With Classified Lists. With 30 Illustrations. 8vo. 16s.

MOORE & JACKMAN on the Clematis as a Garden Flower. Descriptions of the Hardy Species and Varieties, with Directions for their Cultivation. 8vo. 10s. 6d

MOORE'S (Thomas) Life and Letters of Lord Byron. *Cabinet Edition.* With Plates. 6 Vols. Fcap. 8vo. 18s.; *Popular Edition,* with Portraits. Royal 8vo. 7s. 6d.

MOSSMAN'S (Samuel) New Japan; the Land of the Rising Sun; its Annals and Progress during the past Twenty Years, recording the remarkable Progress of the Japanese in Western Civilisation. With Map. 8vo. 15s.

MOTLEY'S (J. L.) History of the United Netherlands: from the Death of William the Silent to the Twelve Years' Truce, 1609. *Library Edition.* Portraits. 4 Vols. 8vo. 60s. *Cabinet Edition.* 4 Vols. Post 8vo. 6s. each.

———————————— Life and Death of John of Barneveld, Advocate of Holland. With a View of the Primary Causes and Movements of the Thirty Years' War. *Library Edition.* Illustrations. 2 Vols. 8vo. 28s. *Cabinet Edition.* 2 vols. Post 8vo. 12s.

MOUHOT'S (Henri) Siam, Cambojia, and Lao; a Narrative of Travels and Discoveries. Illustrations. 2 Vols. 8vo.

MOZLEY'S (Canon) Treatise on Predestination. 8vo. 14s.

———————— Primitive Doctrine of Baptismal Regeneration. 8vo. 7s. 6d.

MUIRHEAD'S (Jas.) Vaux-de-Vire of Maistre Jean Le Houx, Advocate of Vire. Translated and Edited. With Portrait and Illustrations. 8vo.

MUNRO'S (General) Life and Letters. By Rev. G. R. Gleig. Post 8vo. 3s. 6d.

MURCHISON'S (Sir Roderick) Siluria; or, a History of the Oldest rocks containing Organic Remains. Map and Plates. 8vo. 18s.

———————— Memoirs. With Notices of his Contemporaries, and Rise and Progress of Palæozoic Geology. By Archibald Geikie. Portraits. 2 Vols. 8vo. 30s.

MURRAY'S RAILWAY READING. Containing:—

Wellington. By Lord Ellesmere. 6d.	Mahon's Joan of Arc. 1s.
Nimrod on the Chase. 1s.	Head's Emigrant. 2s. 6d.
Music and Dress. 1s	Nimrod on the Road. 1s.
Milman's Fall of Jerusalem. 1s.	Croker on the Guillotine. 1s.
Mahon's "Forty-Five." 3s.	Hollway's Norway. 2s.
Life of Theodore Hook. 1s.	Maure's Wellington. 1s. 6d.
Deeds of Naval Daring. 3s. 6d.	Campbell's Life of Bacon. 2s. 6d.
The Honey Bee. 1s.	The Flower Garden. 1s.
Æsop's Fables. 2s. 6d.	Taylor's Notes from Life. 2s
Nimrod on the Turf. 1s. 6d.	Rejected Addresses. 1s
Art of Dining. 1s. 6d.	Penn's Hints on Angling. 1s

MUSTERS' (Capt.) Patagonians; a Year's Wanderings over Untrodden Ground from the Straits of Magellan to the Rio Negro. Illustrations. Post 8vo. 7s. 6d.

NAPIER'S (Sir Chas.) Life, Journals, and Letters. Portraits. 4 Vols. Crown 8vo. 48s.

———————— (Sir Wm.) Life and Letters. Portraits. 2 Vols. Crown 8vo. 28s.

———————— English Battles and Sieges of the Peninsular War. Portrait. Post 8vo. 9s.

NAPOLEON at Fontainebleau and Elba. A Journal of Occurrences and Notes of Conversations. By Sir N. H. Campbell, C.B. With a Memoir. By Rev. A. N. C. Maclachlan, M.A. Portrait. 8vo. 15s.

NASMYTH and CARPENTER. The Moon. Considered as a Planet, a World, and a Satellite. With Illustrations from Drawings made with the aid of Powerful Telescopes, Woodcuts, &c. 4to. 30s.

NAUTICAL ALMANAC (THE). (*By Authority.*) 2s. 6d.

NAVY LIST. (Monthly and Quarterly.) Post 8vo.

NEW TESTAMENT. With Short Explanatory Commentary.
By ARCHDEACON CHURTON, M.A., and ARCHDEACON BASIL JONES, M.A.
With 110 authentic Views, &c. 2 Vols. Crown 8vo 21s. *bound.*

NEWTH'S (SAMUEL) First Book of Natural Philosophy ; an Introduction to the Study of Statics, Dynamics, Hydrostatics, Optics, and
Acoustics, with numerous Examples. Small 8vo. 3s. 6d.

———— Elements of Mechanics, including Hydrostatics,
with numerous Examples. Small 8vo. 8s. 6d.

———— Mathematical Examinations. A Graduated
Series of Elementary Examples in Arithmetic, Algebra, Logarithms,
Trigonometry, and Mechanics. Small 8vo. 8s. 6d.

NICHOLS' (J. G.) Pilgrimages to Walsingham and Canterbury.
By ERASMUS. Translated, with Notes. With Illustrations. Post 8vo. 6s.

———— (SIR GEORGE) History of the English, Irish and
Scotch Poor Laws. 4 Vols. 8vo.

NICOLAS' (SIR HARRIS) Historic Peerage of England. Exhi-
biting the Origin, Descent, and Present State of every Title of Peerage which has existed in this Country since the Conquest. By
WILLIAM COURTHOPE. 8vo. 30s.

NIMROD, On the Chace—Turf—and Road. With Portrait and
Plates. Crown 8vo. 5s. Or with Coloured Plates, 7s. 6d.

NORDHOFF'S (CHAS) Communistic Societies of the United
States ; including Detailed Accounts of the Shakers, The Amana,
Oneida, Bethell, Aurora, Icarian and other existing Societies; with
Particulars of their Religious Creeds, Industries, and Present Condi-
tion. With 40 Illustrations. 8vo. 15s.

OLD LONDON ; Papers read at the Archæological Institute.
By various Authors. 8vo. 12s.

ORMATHWAITE'S (LORD) Astronomy and Geology—Darwin and
Buckle—Progress and Civilisation. Crown 8vo. 6s.

OWEN'S (LIEUT.-COL.) Principles and Practice of Modern Artillery,
including Artillery Material, Gunnery, and Organisation and Use of
Artillery in Warfare. With Illustrations. 8vo. 15s.

OXENHAM'S (REV. W.) English Notes for Latin Elegiacs ; designed
for early Proficients in the Art of Latin Versification, with Prefatory
Rules of Composition in Elegiac Metre. 12mo. 3s. 6d.

PALGRAVE'S (R. H. I.) Local Taxation of Great Britain and
Ireland. 8vo. 5s.

———— NOTES ON BANKING IN GREAT BRITAIN AND IRE-
LAND, SWEDEN, DENMARK, AND HAMBURG, with some Remarks on
the amount of Bills in circulation both Inland and Foreign. 8vo. 6s.

PALLISER'S (MRS.) Brittany and its Byeways, its Inhabitants,
and Antiquities. With Illustrations. Post 8vo. 12s.

———— Mottoes for Monuments, or Epitaphs selected for
General Use and Study. With Illustrations. Crown 8vo. 7s. 6d.

PARIS' (DR.) Philosophy in Sport made Science in Earnest ;
or, the First Principles of Natural Philosophy inculcated by aid of the
Toys and Sports of Youth. Woodcuts. Post 8vo. 7s. 6d.

PARKMAN'S (FRANCIS) Discovery of the Great West ; or, The
Valleys of the Mississippi and the Lakes of North America. An
Historical Narrative. Map. 8vo. 10s. 6d.

PARKYNS' (MANSFIELD) Three Years' Residence in Abyssinia :
with Travels in that Country. With Illustrations. Post 8vo. 7s. 6d.

PEEK PRIZE ESSAYS. The Maintenance of the Church of
England as an Established Church. By REV. CHARLES HOLE—REV.
R. WATSON DIXON —and REV. JULIUS LLOYD. 8vo. 10s. 6d.

PEEL'S (SIR ROBERT) Memoirs. 2 Vols. Post 8vo. 15s.

PENN'S (RICHARD) Maxims and Hints for an Angler and Chess-player. Woodcuts. Fcap. 8vo. 1s.

PERCY'S (JOHN, M.D.) Metallurgy. Vol. I., Part .1. FUEL, Wood, Peat, Coal, Charcoal, Coke, Refractory Materials, Fire-Clays, &c. With Illustrations. 8vo. 30s.

———— Vol. I., Part 2. Copper, Zinc, Brass. With Illustrations. 8vo [In the Press.

———— Vol. II. Iron and Steel. With Illustrations. 8vo. [In Preparation.

———— Vol. III. Lead, including part of SILVER. With Illustrations. 8vo. 30s.

———— Vols. IV. and V. Gold, Silver, and Mercury, Platinum, Tin, Nickel, Cobalt. Antimony, Bismuth, Arsenic, and other Metals. With Illustrations. 8vo. [In Preparation.

PERSIA'S (SHAH OF) Diary during his Tour through Europe in 1873. Translated from the Original. By J. W. REDHOUSE. With Portrait and Coloured Title. Crown 8vo. 12s.

PHILLIPS' (JOHN) Memoirs of William Smith. 8vo. 7s. 6d.

———— Geology of Yorkshire, The Coast, and Limestone District. Plates. 2 Vols. 4to.

———— Rivers, Mountains, and Sea Coast of Yorkshire. With Essays on the Climate, Scenery, and Ancient Inhabitants. Plates. 8vo. 15s.

———— (SAMUEL) Literary Essays from "The Times." With Portrait. 2 Vols. Fcap. 8vo. 7s.

POPE'S (ALEXANDER) Works. With Introductions and Notes, by REV. WHITWELL ELWIN. Vols. I., II., VI., VII., VIII. With Portraits. 8vo. 10s. 6d. each.

PORTER'S (REV. J. L.) Damascus, Palmyra, and Lebanon. With Travels among the Giant Cities of Bashan and the Hauran. Map and Woodcuts. Post 8vo. 7s. 6d.

PRAYER-BOOK (ILLUSTRATED), with Borders, Initials, Vignettes, &c. Edited, with Notes, by REV. THOS. JAMES. Medium 8vo. 18s. cloth ; 31s. 6d calf ; 36s. morocco.

PRINCESS CHARLOTTE OF WALES. A Brief Memoir. With Selections from her Correspondence and other unpublished Papers. By LADY ROSE WEIGALL. With Portrait. 8vo. 8s. 6d.

PUSS 'IN BOOTS. With 12 Illustrations. By OTTO SPECKTER. 16mo. 1s. 6d. Or coloured, 2s. 6d.

PRINCIPLES AT STAKE. Essays on Church Questions of the Day. 8vo. 12s. Contents :—

Ritualism and Uniformity.—Benjamin Shaw.
The Episcopate.—Bishop of Bath and Wells.
The Priesthood.—Dean of Canterbury.
National Education.—Rev. Alexander R. Grant.
Doctrine of the Eucharist.—Rev. G. H. Sumner.

Scripture and Ritual.—Canon Bernard.
Church in South Africa.—Arthur Mills.
Schismatical Tendency of Ritualism. —Rev. Dr. Salmon.
Revisions of the Liturgy.—Rev. W. G. Humphry.
Parties and Party Spirit.—Dean of Chester.

PRIVY COUNCIL JUDGMENTS in Ecclesiastical Cases relating to Doctrine and Discipline. With Historical Introduction, by G. C. BRODRICK and W. H. FREMANTLE. 8vo. 10s. 6d.

QUARTERLY REVIEW (THE). 8vo. 6s.

RAE'S (EDWARD) Land of the North Wind ; or Travels among the Laplanders and Samoyedes, and along the Shores of the White Sea. With Map and Woodcuts. Post 8vo. 10s. 6d.

RAMBLES in the Syrian Deserts. Post 8vo. 10s. 6d.

RANKE'S (LEOPOLD) History of the Popes of Rome during the 16th and 17th Centuries. Translated from the German by SARAH AUSTIN. 3 Vols. 8vo. 30s.

RASSAM'S (HORMUZD) Narrative of the British Mission to Abyssinia. With Notices of the Countries Traversed from Massowah to Magdala. Illustrations. 2 Vols. 8vo. 28s.

RAWLINSON'S (CANON) Herodotus. A New English Version. Edited with Notes and Essays. Maps and Woodcut. 4 Vols. 8vo. 48s.

———————— Five Great Monarchies of Chaldæa, Assyria, Media, Babylonia, and Persia. With Maps and Illustrations. 3 Vols. 8vo. 42s.

———————— (SIR HENRY) England and Russia in the East; a Series of Papers on the Political and Geographical Condition of Central Asia. Map 8vo. 12s.

REED'S (E. J.) Shipbuilding in Iron and Steel; a Practical Treatise, giving full details of Construction, Processes of Manufacture, and Building Arrangements. With 5 Plans and 250 Woodcuts. 8vo.

———————— Iron - Clad Ships; their Qualities, Performances, and Cost. With Chapters on Turret Ships, Iron-Clad Rams, &c. With Illustrations. 8vo. 12s.

REJECTED ADDRESSES (THE). By JAMES AND HORACE SMITH. Woodcuts Post 8vo. 3s. 6d.; or Popular Edition, Fcap. 8vo. 1s.

RESIDENCE IN BULGARIA; or, Notes on the Resources and Administration of Turkey, &c. By S. G. B. ST. CLAIR and CHARLES A. BROPHY. 8vo. 12s.

REYNOLDS' (SIR JOSHUA) Life and Times. By C. R. LESLIE, R.A. and TOM TAYLOR. Portraits. 2 Vols. 8vo.

RICARDO'S (DAVID) Political Works. With a Notice of his Life and Writings. By J. R. M'CULLOCH. 8vo. 16s.

RIPA'S (FATHER) Thirteen Years' Residence at the Court of Peking. Post 8vo. 2s.

ROBERTSON'S (CANON) History of the Christian Church, from the Apostolic Age to the Reformation, 1517 Library Edition. 4 Vols. 8vo. Cabinet Edition. 8 Vols. Post 8vo. 6s. each.

———————— How shall we Conform to the Liturgy. 12mo. 9s.

ROME. See LIDDELL and SMITH.

ROWLAND'S (DAVID) Manual of the English Constitution. Its Rise, Growth, and Present State. Post 8vo. 10s. 6d.

———————— Laws of Nature the Foundation of Morals. Post 8vo. 6s.

ROBSON'S (E. R.) SCHOOL ARCHITECTURE. Being Practical Remarks on the Planning, Designing, Building, and Furnishing of School-houses. With 300 Illustrations. Medium 8vo. 31s. 6d.

RUNDELL'S (MRS.) Modern Domestic Cookery. Fcap. 8vo. 5s.

RUXTON'S (GEORGE F.) Travels in Mexico; with Adventures among the Wild Tribes and Animals of the Prairies and Rocky Mountains. Post 8vo. 3s. 6d.

ROBINSON'S (REV. DR.) Biblical Researches in Palestine and the Adjacent Regions, 1838—52. Maps. 3 Vols. 8vo. 42s.

———————— Physical Geography of the Holy Land. Post 8vo. 10s. 6d.

———————— (WM.) Alpine Flowers for English Gardens. With 70 Illustrations. Crown 8vo. 12s.

———————— Wild Gardens; or, our Groves and Shrubberies made beautiful by the Naturalization of Hardy Exotic Plants. With Frontispiece. Small 8vo. 6s.

———————— Sub-Tropical Gardens; or, Beauty of Form in the Flower Garden. With Illustrations. Small 8vo. 7s. 6d.

SALE'S (Sir Robert) Brigade in Affghanistan. With an Account of the Defence of Jellalabad. By Rev. G. R. Gleig. Post 8vo. 2s.

SCHLIEMANN'S (Dr. Henry) Troy and Its Remains. A Narrative of Researches and Discoveries made on the Site of Ilium and the Trojan Plain. Edited by Philip Smith, B.A. With Maps, Views, and 500 Illustrations. Medium 8vo. 42s.

SCOTT'S (Sir G. G.) Secular and Domestic Architecture, Present and Future. 8vo. 9s.

———— (Dean) University Sermons. Post 8vo. 8s. 6d.

SHADOWS OF A SICK ROOM. With a Preface by Canon Liddon. 16mo. 2s 6d.

SCROPE'S (G. P.) Geology and Extinct Volcanoes of Central France. Illustrations. Medium 8vo. 30s.

SHAW'S (T. B.) Manual of English Literature. Post 8vo. 7s. 6d.

———— Specimens of English Literature. Selected from the Chief Writers. Post 8vo. 7s. 6d.

———— (Robert) Visit to High Tartary, Yarkand, and Kashgar (formerly Chinese Tartary), and Return Journey over the Karakorum Pass. With Map and Illustrations. 8vo. 16s.

SHIRLEY'S (Evelyn P.) Deer and Deer Parks; or some Account of English Parks, with Notes on the Management of Deer. Illustrations. 4to. 21s.

SIERRA LEONE; Described in Letters to Friends at Home. By A Lady. Post 8vo. 3s. 6d.

SINCLAIR'S (Archdeacon) Old Times and Distant Places. A Series of Sketches. Crown 8vo. 9s.

SMILES' (Samuel) British Engineers; from the Earliest Period to the death of the Stephensons. With Illustrations. 5 Vols. Crown 8vo. 7s. 6d. each.

———— George and Robert Stephenson. Illustrations. Medium 8vo. 21s.

———— Boulton and Watt. Illustrations. Medium 8vo. 21s.

———— Self-Help. With Illustrations of Conduct and Perseverance. Post 8vo. 6s. Or in French, 6s.

———— Character. A Sequel to "Self-Help." Post 8vo. 6s.

———— Thrift. A Companion Volume to "Self-Help" and "Character." Post 8vo. 6s.

———— Boy's Voyage round the World. With Illustrations. Post 8vo. 6s.

STANLEY'S (Dean) Sinai and Palestine, in connexon with their History. 20th Thousand. Map. 8vo. 14s

———— Bible in the Holy Land; Extracted from the above Work. Second Edition. Woodcuts. Fcap. 8vo. 2s. 6d.

———— Eastern Church. Fourth Edition. Plans. 8vo. 12s.

———— Jewish Church. 1st & 2nd Series. From the Earliest Times to the Captivity 8vo. 24s.

———— Third Series. From the Captivity to the Destruction of Jerusalem. 8vo.

———— Church of Scotland. 8vo. 7s. 6d.

———— Memorials of Canterbury Cathedral. Woodcuts. Post 8vo. 7s. 6d.

———— Westminster Abbey. With Illustrations. 8vo. 21s.

———— Sermons during a Tour in the East. 8vo. 9s.

———— Addresses and Charges of the late Bishop Stanley. With Memoir. 8vo. 10s. 6d.

———— Epistles of St. Paul to the Corinthians. 8vo. 18s

SMITH'S (Dr. Wm) Dictionary of the Bible; its Antiquities, Biography, Geography, and Natural History. Illustrations. 3 Vols. 8vo. 105s.

———— Concise Bible Dictionary. With 300 Illustrations. Medium 8vo. 21s.

———— Smaller Bible Dictionary. With Illustrations. Post 8vo. 7s. 6d.

———— Christian Antiquities. Comprising the History, Institutions, and Antiquities of the Christian Church. With Illustrations. Vol. I. 8vo. 31s. 6d.

———— ———— Biography and Doctrines; from the Times of the Apostles to the Age of Charlemagne. 8vo. [In Preparation.

———— Atlas of Ancient Geography—Biblical and Classical. Folio. 6l 6s.

———— Greek and Roman Antiquities. With 500 Illustrations. Medium 8vo. 28s.

———— Biography and Mythology. With 600 Illustrations. 3 Vols. Medium 8vo. 4l. 4s

———— Geography. 2 Vols. With 500 Illustrations. Medium 8vo. 56s.

———— Classical Dictionary of Mythology, Biography, and Geography. 1 Vol. With 750 Woodcuts. 8vo. 18s.

———— Smaller Classical Dictionary. With 200 Woodcuts. Crown 8vo. 7s. 6d.

———— Greek and Roman Antiquities. With 200 Woodcuts. Crown 8vo. 7s. 6d.

———— Latin-English Dictionary. With Tables of the Roman Calendar, Measures, Weights, and Money. Medium 8vo. 21s.

———— Smaller Latin-English Dictionary. 12mo. 7s. 6d.

———— English-Latin Dictionary. Medium 8vo. 21s.

———— Smaller English Latin Dictionary. 12mo. 7s. 6d.

———— School Manual of English Grammar, with Copious Exercises. Post 8vo. 3s. 6d.

———— Modern Geography. 12mo. [Nearly ready.

———— Primary English Grammar. 12mo. 1s.

———— History of Britain. 12mo. 2s. 6d.

———— French Principia. Part I. A First Course, containing a Grammar, Delectus, Exercises, and Vocabularies. 12mo. 3s. 6d.

———— Part II. A Reading Book, containing Fables, Stories, and Anecdotes, Natural History, and Scenes from the History of France. With Grammatical Questions, Notes and copious Etymological Dictionary. 12mo. 4s. 6d.

———— Part III. Prose Composition, containing a Systematic Course of Exercises on the Syntax, with the Principal Rules of Syntax. 12mo. [In the Press.

———— German Principia, Part I. A First German Course, containing a Grammar, Delectus, Exercise Book, and Vocabularies. 12mo. 3s. 6d.

———— Part II. A Reading Book; containing Fables, Stories, and Anecdotes, Natural History, and Scenes from the History of Germany. With Grammatical Questions, Notes, and Dictionary. 12mo. 3s. 6d.

———— Part III. An Introduction to German Prose Composition; containing a Systematic Course of Exercises on the Syntax, with the Principal Rules of Syntax. 12mo. [In the Press.

SMITH'S (Dr. Wm.) Principia Latina—Part I. First Latin Course, containing a Grammar, Delectus, and Exercise Book, with Vocabularies. 12mo. 3s. 6d.
In this Edition the Cases of the Nouns, Adjectives, and Pronouns are arranged both as in the ORDINARY GRAMMARS and as in the PUBLIC SCHOOL PRIMER, together with the corresponding Exercises.

———— Part II. A Reading-book, of Mythology, Geography, Roman Antiquities, and History. With Notes and Dictionary. 12mo. 3s. 6d.

———— Part III. A Poetry Book. Hexameters and Pentameters; Eclog. Ovidianæ; Latin Prosody. 12mo. 3s. 6d.

———— Part IV. Prose Composition. Rules of Syntax with Examples, Explanations of Synonyms, and Exercises on the Syntax. 12mo. 3s. 6d.

———— Part V. Short Tales and Anecdotes for Translation into Latin. 12mo. 3s.

———— Latin-English Vocabulary and First Latin-English Dictionary for Phædrus, Cornelius Nepos, and Cæsar. 12mo. 3s. 6d.

———— Student's Latin Grammar. Post 8vo. 6s.

———— Smaller Latin Grammar. 12mo. 3s. 6d.

———— Tacitus, Germania, Agricola, &c. With English Notes. 12mo. 3s. 6d.

———— Initia Græca, Part I. A First Greek Course, containing a Grammar, Delectus, and Exercise-book. With Vocabularies. 12mo. 3s. 6d.

———— Part II. A Reading Book. Containing Short Tales, Anecdotes, Fables, Mythology, and Grecian History. 12mo. 3s. 6d.

———— Part III. Prose Composition. Containing the Rules of Syntax, with copious Examples and Exercises. 12mo. 3s. 6d.

———— Student's Greek Grammar. By PROFESSOR CURTIUS. Post 8vo. 6s.

———— Smaller Greek Grammar. 12mo. 3s. 6d.

———— Greek Accidence. Extracted from the above work. 12mo. 2s. 6d.

———— Plato. The Apology of Socrates, the Crito, and Part of the Phædo; with Notes in English from Stallbaum and Schleiermacher's Introductions. 12mo. 3s. 6d.

———— Smaller Scripture History. Woodcuts. 16mo. 3s. 6d.

———— Ancient History. Woodcuts. 16mo. 3s. 6d.

———— Geography. Woodcuts. 16mo. 3s. 6d.

———— Rome. Woodcuts. 16mo. 3s. 6d.

———— Greece. Woodcuts. 16mo. 3s. 6d.

———— Classical Mythology. Woodcuts 16mo. 3s. 6d.

———— History of England. Woodcuts. 16mo. 3s. 6d.

———— English Literature. 16mo. 3s. 6d.

———— Specimens of English Literature. 16mo. 3s. 6d.

———— (PHILIP) History of the Ancient World, from the Creation to the Fall of the Roman Empire, A.D. 455. Fourth Edition. 3 Vols. 8vo. 31s. 6d.

———— (REV. A. C.) Nile and its Banks. Woodcuts. 2 Vols. Post 8vo. 18s.

SIMMONS'. (CAPT.) Constitution and Practice of Courts-Martial. Seventh Edition. 8vo. 15s.

STUDENT'S OLD TESTAMENT HISTORY; from the Creation to the Return of the Jews from Captivity. Maps and Woodcuts. Post 8vo. 7s. 6d.

———— **NEW TESTAMENT HISTORY.** With an Introduction connecting the History of the Old and New Testaments. Maps and Woodcuts. Post 8vo. 7s. 6d.

———— **ECCLESIASTICAL HISTORY.** A History of the Christian Church from its Foundation to the Eve of the Protestant Reformation. Post 8vo. 7s. 6d.

———— **ANCIENT HISTORY OF THE EAST**; Egypt, Assyria, Babylonia, Media, Persia, Asia Minor, and Phœnicia. Woodcuts. Post 8vo. 7s. 6d.

———— **GEOGRAPHY.** By Rev. W. L. Bevan. Woodcuts. Post 8vo. 7s. 6d.

———— **HISTORY OF GREECE**; from the Earliest Times to the Roman Conquest. By Wm. Smith, D.C.L. Woodcuts. Crown 8vo. 7s. 6d.
*** Questions on the above Work, 12mo. 2s.

———— **HISTORY OF ROME**; from the Earliest Times to the Establishment of the Empire. By Dean Liddell. Woodcuts. Crown 8vo. 7s. 6d.

———— **GIBBON'S** Decline and Fall of the Roman Empire. Woodcuts. Post 8vo. 7s. 6d.

———— **HALLAM'S HISTORY OF EUROPE** during the Middle Ages. Post 8vo. 7s. 6d.

———— **HALLAM'S HISTORY OF ENGLAND**; from the Accession of Henry VII. to the Death of George II. Post 8vo. 7s. 6d.

———— **HUME'S** History of England from the Invasion of Julius Cæsar to the Revolution in 1688. Continued down to 1868. Woodcuts. Post 8vo. 7s. 6d.
*** Questions on the above Work, 12mo. 2s.

———— **HISTORY OF FRANCE**; from the Earliest Times to the Establishment of the Second Empire, 1852. By Rev. H. W. Jervis. Woodcuts. Post 8vo. 7s. 6d.

———— **ENGLISH LANGUAGE.** By Geo. P. Marsh. Post 8vo. 7s. 6d.

———— **LITERATURE.** By T. B. Shaw, M.A. Post 8vo. 7s. 6d.

———— **SPECIMENS** of English Literature from the Chief Writers. By T. B. Shaw. Post 8vo. 7s. 6d.

———— **MODERN GEOGRAPHY**; Mathematical, Physical, and Descriptive. By Rev. W. L. Bevan. Woodcuts. Post 8vo. 7s. 6d.

———— **MORAL PHILOSOPHY.** By William Fleming, D.D. Post 8vo. 7s. 6d.

———— **BLACKSTONE'S** Commentaries on the Laws of England. By R. Malcolm Kerr, LL.D. Post 8vo. 7s. 6d.

SPALDING'S (Captain) Tale of Frithiof. Translated from the Swedish of Esias Tegner. Post 8vo. 7s. 6d.

STEPHEN'S (Rev. W. R.) Life and Times of St. Chrysostom. With Portrait. 8vo. 15s.

ST. JAMES (The) LECTURES. Companions for the Devout Life. By the following authors. 8vo. 7s. 6d.
Imitation of Christ. Rev. Dr. Farrar.
Pascal's Pensees. Dean Church.
S. François de Sales. Dean Goulbourn.
Baxter's Saints' Rest. Archbishop Trench.
S. Augustine's Confessions. Bishop Alexander.
Jeremy Taylor's Holy Living and Dying. Rev. Dr. Humphry

ST. JOHN'S (CHARLES) Wild Sports and Natural History of the Highlands. Post 8vo. 3s. 6d.

———— (BAYLE) Adventures in the Libyan Desert. Post 8vo. 2s.

STORIES FOR DARLINGS. With Illustrations. 16mo. 5s.

STREET'S (G. E.) Gothic Architecture in Spain. From Personal Observations made during several Journeys. With Illustrations. Royal 8vo. 30s.

———————————————— in Italy, chiefly in Brick and Marble. With Notes of Tours in the North of Italy. With 60 Illustrations. Royal 8vo. 26s.

STANHOPE'S (EARL) England during the Reign of Queen Anne, 1701—13. Library Edition. 8vo. 16s. Cabinet Edition. Portrait. 2 Vols. Post 8vo. 10s.

———————————————— from the Peace of Utrecht to the Peace of Versailles, 1713-83. Library Edition. 7 vols. 8vo. 93s. Cabinet Edition, 7 vols. Post 8vo. 5s. each.

———————————— British India, from its Origin to 1783. 8vo. 3s. 6d.

———————————— History of "Forty-Five." Post 8vo. 3s.

———————————— Historical and Critical Essays. Post 8vo. 3s. 6d.

———————————— Life of Belisarius. Post 8vo. 10s. 6d.

———————————— Condé. Post 8vo. 3s. 6d.

———————————— William Pitt. Portraits. 4 Vols. 8vo. 21s.

———————— Miscellanies. 2 Vols. Post 8vo. 13s.

———————— Story of Joan of Arc. Fcap. 8vo. 1s.

———— Addresses Delivered on Various Occasions. 16mo. 1s.

STYFFE'S (KNUTT) Strength of Iron and Steel. Plates. 8vo. 12s.

SOMERVILLE'S (MARY) Personal Recollections from Early Life to Old Age. With Selections from her Correspondence. Portrait. Crown 8vo. 12s.

———————————— Physical Geography. Portrait. Post 8vo.

———————————— Connexion of the Physical Sciences. Portrait. Post 8vo.

———————————— Molecular and Microscopic Science. Illustrations. 2 Vols. Post 8vo. 21s.

SOUTHEY'S (ROBERT) Book of the Church. Post 8vo. 7s. 6d.
Lives of Bunyan and Cromwell. Post 8vo. 2s.

SWAINSON'S (CANON) Nicene and Apostles' Creeds; Their Literary History; together with some Account of "The Creed of St. Athanasius." 8vo.

SYBEL'S (VON) History of Europe during the French Revolution, 1789—1795. 4 Vols. 8vo. 48s.

SYMONDS' (REV. W.) Records of the Rocks; or Notes on the Geology, Natural History, and Antiquities of North and South Wales, Siluria, Devon, and Cornwall. With Illustrations. Crown 8vo. 12s.

TAYLOR'S (SIR HENRY) Notes from Life. Fcap. 8vo. 2s.

THIELMAN'S (BARON) Journey through the Caucasus to Tabreez, Kurdistan, down the Tigris and Euphrates to Nineveh and Babylon, and across the Desert to Palmyra. Translated by CHAS. HENEAGE. Illustrations. 2 Vols. Post 8vo. 18s.

THOMS' (W. J.) Longevity of Man; its Facts and its Fiction. Including Observations on the more Remarkable Instances. Post 8vo. 10s. 6d.

THOMSON'S (ARCHBISHOP) Lincoln's Inn Sermons. 8vo. 10s. 6d.

———————————— Life in the Light of God's Word. Post 8vo. 5s.

TOCQUEVILLE'S State of Society in France before the Revolution, 1789, and on the Causes which led to that Event. Translated by HENRY REEVE. 8vo. 12s.

TOMLINSON (CHARLES); The Sonnet; Its Origin, Structure, and Place in Poetry. With translations from Dante, Petrarch, &c. Post 8vo. 9s.

TOZER'S (REV. H. F.) Highlands of Turkey, with Visits to Mounts Ida, Athos, Olympus, and Pelion. 2 Vols. Crown 8vo. 24s.

——————— Lectures on the Geography of Greece. Map. Post 8vo. 9s.

TRISTRAM'S (CANON) Great Sahara. Illustrations. Crown 8vo. 15s.

——————— Land of Moab; Travels and Discoveries on the East Side of the Dead Sea and the Jordan. Illustrations. Crown 8vo. 15s.

TWISLETON (EDWARD). The Tongue not Essential to Speech, with Illustrations of the Power of Speech in the case of the African Confessors. Post 8vo. 6s.

TWISS' (HORACE) Life of Lord Eldon. 2 Vols. Post 8vo. 21s.

TYLOR'S (E. B.) Early History of Mankind, and Development of Civilization. 8vo. 12s.

——————— Primitive Culture; the Development of Mythology, Philosophy, Religion, Art, and Custom. 2 Vols. 8vo. 24s.

VAMBERY'S (ARMINIUS) Travels from Teheran across the Turko-man Desert on the Eastern Shore of the Caspian. Illustrations. 8vo. 21s.

VAN LENNEP'S (HENRY J.) Travels in Asia Minor. With Illustrations of Biblical Literature, and Archaeology. With Woodcuts. 2 Vols. Post 8vo. 24s.

——————— Modern Customs and Manners of Bible Lands, in illustration of Scripture. With Maps and 300 Illustrations. 2 Vols. 8vo. 21s.

WELLINGTON'S Despatches during his Campaigns in India, Denmark, Portugal, Spain, the Low Countries, and France. Edited by COLONEL GURWOOD. 8 Vols. 8vo. 20s. each.

—— Supplementary Despatches, relating to India, Ireland, Denmark, Spanish America, Spain, Portugal, France, Congress of Vienna, Waterloo and Paris. Edited by his SON. 14 Vols. 8vo. 20s. each. *,* An Index. 8vo. 20s.

——————— Civil and Political Correspondence. Edited by his SON. Vols. I. to V. 8vo. 20s. each.

——————— Despatches (Selections from). 8vo. 18s.

——————— Speeches in Parliament. 2 Vols. 8vo. 42s.

WHEELER'S (G.) Choice of a Dwelling; a Practical Handbook of Useful Information on Building a House. Plans. Post 8vo. 7s. 6d.

WHYMPER'S (FREDERICK) Travels and Adventures in Alaska. Illustrations. 8vo. 16s.

WILBERFORCE'S (BISHOP) Essays on Various Subjects. 2 vols. 8vo. 21s.

——————— Life of William Wilberforce. Portrait. Crown 8vo. 6s.

WILKINSON'S (SIR J. G.) Popular Account of the Ancient Egyptians. With 500 Woodcuts. 2 Vols. Post 8vo. 12s.

WOOD'S (CAPTAIN) Source of the Oxus. With the Geography of the Valley of the Oxus. By COL. YULE. Map. 8vo. 12s.

WORDS OF HUMAN WISDOM. Collected and Arranged by E. S. With a Preface by CANON LIDDON. Fcap. 8vo. 3s. 6d.

WORDSWORTH'S (BISHOP) Athens and Attica. Plates. 8vo. 5s.

——————— Greece. With 600 Woodcuts. Royal 8vo.

YULE'S (COLONEL) Book of Marco Polo. Illustrated by the Light of Oriental Writers and Modern Travels. With Maps and 80 Plates. 2 Vols. Medium 8vo. 63s.